School Choice and the Future of American Democracy

School Choice and the
Future of American Democracy

Scott Franklin Abernathy

The University of Michigan Press

Ann Arbor

2008   2007   2006   2005   4   3   2   1

A CIP catalog record for this book is available from the British Library.

Library of Congress Cataloging-in-Publication Data

Abernathy, Scott Franklin, 1966–
    School choice and the future of American democracy / Scott
Franklin Abernathy.
        p.   cm.
    Includes bibliographical references and index.
    ISBN-13: 978-0-472-09901-6 (cloth : alk. paper)
    ISBN-10: 0-472-09901-9 (cloth : alk. paper)
    ISBN-13: 978-0-472-06901-9 (pbk. : alk. paper)
    ISBN-10: 0-472-06901-2 (pbk. : alk. paper)
    1. School choice—United States.   2. Educational vouchers—
United States.   3. Charter schools—United States.   4. Educational
equalization—United States.   5. Education—Political aspects—
United States.   I. Title.

LB1027.9.A24   2006
379.1'11'0973—dc22   2005006879

For Sara
In memory of Arthur, Rita, and Russell

Contents

Acknowledgments

I WOULD LIKE TO THANK MY DISSERTATION ADVISERS: R. Douglas Arnold, Larry M. Bartels, and Jennifer L. Hochschild. At each step of the process, Doug, Larry, and Jennifer guided and often pushed me to go beyond what I thought I could do. Graduate students are, in many ways, the interaction terms of their advisers, combining diverse thoughts and approaches in trying to make something of their own. The care and thoughtfulness of these three individuals have helped make this project much more than would have been possible otherwise and have made me feel very, very fortunate. I owe so much to all of them, but especially to Doug.

I would also like to offer special thanks to Lawrence R. Jacobs of the University of Minnesota and to anonymous reviewers of the manuscript. Their comments and suggestions were crucial in framing the arguments that transformed the dissertation into a book. Any mistakes and omissions are mine alone.

I would like to thank the graduate students, faculty, and staff of the Politics Department at Princeton University for their guidance, suggestions, and assistance over the years. In particular, I would like to thank Jameson Doig, Fred Greenstein, Christopher Mackie, Tali Mendelberg, Nathan Scovronick, Thomas Romer, Christa Scholtz, and Keith Whittington. At the University of Minnesota, I am indebted to pretty much everybody for their help, suggestions, commiseration, and/or encouragement. For specific advice on and suggestions for this project, I would like to thank Christopher Federico, John Freeman, James Farr, Timothy Johnson, Jeffrey Lomonoco, Joanne Miller, Wendy Rahn, and David Samuels.

This research was partially funded through a grant from the University of Minnesota's Center for Urban and Regional Affairs Faculty Interactive Research Program, and I would like to thank Tom Scott, Will Craig, and CURA's staff for their invaluable assistance. I would also like to thank Robert J. Schmidt, Executive Director of the Minnesota Association of

Secondary School Principals, and P. Fred Storti, Executive Director of the Minnesota Elementary School Principals' Association. In addition, I am indebted to Rossana Armson, Pam Jones, and Marc Wagoner from the Minnesota Center for Survey Research and graduate student assistants Angela Bos and Jeff Hubbard.

Many others outside of Minnesota and Princeton have contributed as well, including John J. DiIulio Jr., R. Kenneth Godwin, Sanford Gordon, Jeffrey Henig, Gregory Huber, Jeffrey Lewis, Kenneth Meier, Suzanne Mettler, Robert Maranto, Michael Mintrom, J. Eric Oliver, Mark Schneider, and Paul Teske. I owe much to all of these scholars. I would also like to thank Jim Reische, Amy Anderson, Kevin Rennells, and the staff of the University of Michigan Press for all of their help and assistance.

This project would not have been possible without the generosity of the public school principals in my studies. Though they remain anonymous, I would like to thank them for their commitment, openness, and insight. I would also like to thank my parents. They gave me the 1990 Cadillac DeVille that I used to traverse the highways and byways of New Jersey, and so much more. Finally, I would like to thank the Ramones for "Sheena Is a Punk Rocker." This book would not have been the same without it.

Scott Abernathy
Minneapolis
June 2005

1 | Faith in the Markets

Americans have lost faith in institutions that are the foundations of our democracy. . . . Our principal problems are not
the product of great economic shifts or other vast unforeseen
forces. They are the creation of government, of government
that puts special interests ahead of the people, of government
that refuses to change.

—*Christine Todd Whitman, Governor of New Jersey, Inaugural
Address, 1994*[1]

The market environment that works so well at identifying
winners and losers in business finally will be allowed to work
its magic within the public school system.

—*Duane Wareheime, New Jersey chapter of United We Stand, in
support of Governor Whitman's school voucher proposal*[2]

IT WAS THE FIRST DAY at one of my prospective research sites: a small
public school in an inner city in New Jersey. I was there to talk to the principal, to explain that I wanted to follow her around as she interacted with
parents and community members, to find out what she sees when she
thinks about her parent community, how she is responsive to them, and to
explore how any of this might be changing under the state's four-year-old
school choice program. The visit began—as would all subsequent visits to
this and other schools—in the main office. Sitting on a bench, among the
ebb and flow of adolescents, I noticed, placed on the back wall over a photocopier, the front page of a local newspaper. Its headline read, in four-
inch letters, "Here Comes School Choice!" I wondered if the principal had
put it up. I knew that the district superintendent had embraced school
choice, and I was not interested in the degree to which the poster might sig-
nal her public support for school choice. I was more interested in who else
she might be talking to, and why.

Later, while sitting in her office, I asked the principal about the poster.
"I had a parent that wanted to transfer her child to a charter," she
explained to me. She meant from this public school to a charter school, a

publicly funded school accountable mostly to its charter, its founding document, exempting it from many of the regulatory and collective bargaining constraints she faced in her work every day. The parent and student would be leaving this school, taking thousands of dollars in state aid and local tax dollars to the new charter school. "She came in here to sign the form," the principal continued. "While I had her here, I told her about some of our programs. She left here completely confused. If you don't adapt and change, if you don't markct, well . . . you get what you get."

The great hope of the school choice movement is the possibility that the introduction of market forces will make for more efficient and responsive public educational institutions. Public school monopolists—under competition from charter schools and, perhaps, private schools—will pay more attention to their customers and produce higher quality educational services if they are to survive. This potential for bureaucratic transformation is based on changing the relationship between parents and their public schools. Parents become customers. Public schools become firms that compete in a more private marketplace for those customers.

It is this possibility of bureaucratic transformation that shields school choice from serious challenges on the basis of fairness. We need not worry so much about winners and losers in the new educational marketplace if that marketplace improves the quality of education for all students, even those who do not, or cannot, participate in a school choice program. What is often lost in the school choice debate, however, is that parents are much more than customers. They are also citizens who exert control over education, not by their power in the marketplace, but through their votes on school budgets and through their larger participation in shaping educational policy, from the bake sales to the school board meetings.

In this book I explore what happens to public schools confronting policies designed to transform their citizens into customers. I focus on only a small part of the school choice debate—how school choice reforms affect control over and involvement with the public schools by customers and citizens—but argue that this narrow focus may offer lessons both for school choice reforms and larger questions in the study of private markets and democratic communities. I complicate the crucial assumption that public schools will necessarily improve when confronted with market-based reforms and raise the possibility of more disconnected and isolated public schools under choice, especially if those policies facilitate exit to the private sector rather than providing choices within it.

I begin, therefore, with a question and a puzzle: How will school choice reforms affect the relationship between parents and their schools? What is the connection between the pursuit of individual liberty and the pursuit of democratic equality in education? Choice advocates argue that we need more individual choices in education and less democratic involvement if we are to have academically excellent schools. Opponents fear that facilitating choices will weaken the public commitment to education and benefit a small number of students at the expense of many more. It is possible that either, both, or neither of these arguments is correct or has something to add to our understanding.

Markets and Politics in Education

School choice policies are predicated on the assumption that America's public schools have a politics problem and that they are in need of a market solution. This recent wave of privatization is theoretically rooted in Milton Friedman's suggestion that parents be given vouchers to send their children to the school of their choice, in order to force the educational monopoly to change by allowing parents to vote with their feet.[3] Though Friedman focused on voucher programs, the idea of a market solution to the politics problem has since been extended to a wide range of school choice alternatives, including magnet schools, charter schools, and intradistrict and interdistrict choice programs.

John Chubb and Terry Moe provide the most complete theoretical justification for bringing market solutions to the provision of education. In *Politics, Markets, and America's Schools,* the authors place the blame for America's educational failures squarely at the feet of direct democratic control and its attendant institutions: local school boards, superintendents, and state departments of education.[4] The effects on school quality imposed by these institutions are significant. Democracy leads to bureaucratization, which, in turn, leads to lower quality schools. Given the constraints placed on public schools by systems of direct democratic control, private schools emerge as organizationally and, therefore, pedagogically superior. Though unintended, this consequence is institutionally determined. Any educational reforms short of institutional overhaul, therefore, will not succeed.

Introducing marketlike choices to public education, Chubb and Moe argue, will replace educational bureaucracies with consumer-oriented firms who are more responsive to customer interests and less responsive to the administrative hierarchy. The first critical assumption of their institutionalist perspective is that markets will have the same desirable effects on the public bureaucracy. Even if one assumes that the marketplace creates better private schools, it requires a much stronger set of assumptions to assert that the market will similarly work its magic on a preexisting public bureaucracy without producing other, perhaps unintended, consequences.

The second, and more fundamental, assumption in Chubb and Moe's critique—that one can actually take politics out of the schools—fails to recognize that actors in the policy space operate as participants in both politics and markets. Though we may wish to treat politics and markets separately, we need to rethink the effects of market forces on educational politics in a way that incorporates and accounts for the effects of both on each other.[5] In fact, most of the modern institutions of social welfare provision are neither purely economic nor purely political and cannot be correctly understood that way.[6]

In his book *A Preface to Economic Democracy,* Robert Dahl re-asks the classical political question "Is equality inimical to liberty?"[7] Dahl begins by tracing the Founders' concern with the possibility that equality might damage the expression of liberty in a democratic society. James Madison, Alexander Hamilton, and John Jay, according to Dahl, argued that equality can damage liberty, a point echoed in Chubb and Moe's critique that the institutions of direct democratic control necessarily have deleterious effects on educational quality. Focusing only on the expression of liberty by individuals forms the basis for framing school choice as a conflict between liberty and servitude. Giving choices to parents will free them from the stranglehold of the bureaucratic monopoly.

Dahl's analysis, however, flips the classical question upside down, by arguing that we also need to look the other way and ask if the expression of individual liberty can damage political equality. He concludes that liberty can damage equality, and that this concern is hardly new. The challenge of harnessing the two competing forces of self-interest and public spirit was also of central importance to the framers of the Constitution, who realized that the tension was inherent to the continual enterprise of free government.[8]

This connection between equality and liberty has not been lost on scholars of education policy. Researchers have argued that the tension between individual and community interests is useful in explaining a wide range of debates in educational policy, including desegregation, school funding, bilingual education, and school choice.[9] One of the theoretical critiques of Chubb and Moe's argument, raised by Jeffrey R. Henig in his critique of their market-oriented approach, centered on a concern that the free-market rhetoric might obscure the "required trade-off between choice and other values, such as stability, equity, and community."[10]

If Chubb and Moe follow in classical concern for liberty (educational opportunity) in the presence of institutions designed to protect democratic equality (the institutions of school governance), I take up the concern of Dahl and his followers about the dangers of facilitating individual liberty on the expression of democratic equality. Thinking about school choice policies in this way introduces two other tensions, both closely related: between politics and markets and between citizens and consumers. Understanding the likely effects of choice policies on the larger political context requires a careful consideration of what we mean by citizen and consumer, public and private, and, most important, what it means for the public schools to operate under quasi-public, quasi-private institutional arrangements. Exploring these tensions might give us a deeper understanding of market-based policy reforms, their effects on larger political contexts, and what needs to be done to mitigate the negative consequences of their implementation while attempting to preserve the benefits.

Though there may be efficiency gains to be made from supporting self-interested behavior in education, there may also be significant democratic costs to attaining these potential bureaucratic efficiencies, particularly if these policies—through the provision of vouchers for private schools—privilege the private sector. The source of these costs lies in changes brought about in the expression of political voice through the introduction of market forces as described by Albert Hirschman in *Exit, Voice, and Loyalty.* Hirschman analyzes the conditions under which exit (whereby customers choose other firms) and voice (whereby customers make their grievances known while staying with the firm) interact with and prevail over each other.[11] Exit, to Hirschman, lies within the clean and direct realm of economics. Voice operates in the messier world of politics. The key point is that the market mechanism of exit and the political mechanism of voice need not be mutually exclusive, but typically interact, potentially damaging each other in the process.

Exit is straightforward. One expresses displeasure with the firm by voting with one's feet. The consequences to managers within the firm are clear: Customers are leaving. Changes need to be made. Voice, however, is less direct and more costly. As voice involves problems of collective action and is a more individually burdensome task,[12] the facilitation of exit presents a danger to the expression of voice. It does so primarily through the departure of the most vocal customers, those whose voices could have most effectively constrained the behavior of the abandoned firm. The same customers on whom firms rely for effective voice are also the first to exercise the exit option.

The role of the most vocal customers in the use of voice as a means of bureaucratic control is crucial. These marginal consumers possess the requisite skills, information, and attitudes to have their needs met,[13] and their exercise of exit could result in a concentration of politically active and effective individuals within choice options and away from assigned public schools. The exit of these marginal consumers, Hirschman warns, "paralyzes voice by depriving it of its principal agents."[14]

When voice turns to exit, what is left in its wake? The problematic possibility is quiescence:[15] the most troubled public schools become less constrained and more poorly supported by a parent community that has lost its most active voices to choice options. This possibility, I argue, is the distributional consequence of exit. More speculative is the possibility that the decision to exit from the public schools is accompanied by a change in political participation among the active choosers, who become more private in the application of their newly empowered civic skills and abilities. Albert Hirschman suggested that those who exit might become more privately focused, particularly to the extent that each "customer-member who exits from a public good behaves *as though* he were exiting from a private one."[16]

The replacement of larger political duties and obligations with those of the private sector is the dispositional consequence of exit. This kind of transformation—if restricted to the private sector—has the potential to negatively impact a wide range of institutions involved in democratic control, including turnout in school elections, support for public school budgets, and all of the forms of participation that keep parents connected to their schools and allow the school principals to nurture and use their communities as a resource. Taken together, the distributional and dispositional consequences of exit point to a privatization of voice, whereby the most active and involved members of public institutions exit to the private sector, changing the dynamics of institutional control in their wake and restricting their own understandings of political obligations in the process.

The authors of a study of public school choice in New Jersey and New York noted that the possible drain to individual public schools brought about by siphoning off active and involved parents is "one of the most fundamental criticisms leveled against choice"[17] and "maybe the most critical issue for choice."[18] In spite of the potential consequences of this activist skimming, the authors note that "there is remarkably little evidence in the literature about this issue."[19] I hope to fill in this important gap in our understanding of choice and the public schools.

Hirschman's concern for the loss of voice is central to the related ideas of civic capacity and civic mobilization developed by Clarence Stone and his colleagues in *Building Civic Capacity*. In an endeavor such as education reform that requires a sustained collective commitment to work, the coming together of various sectors of the community (civic mobilization) depends upon a larger capable commitment to the collective enterprise (civic capacity).[20] For Stone and colleagues, exit is a dangerous and viable alternative to civic mobilization. Whereas they focus on the drain brought about by suburbanization, I argue that school choice policies may—if not thoughtfully implemented—have the potential to drain the "effective leadership core around which a political movement for reform might be built."[21]

Like Chubb and Moe, Stone and colleagues' work focuses on the persistent failure of urban school reform, though they come at it from a very different perspective. They ask why urban school reform has failed so spectacularly in spite of much attention and energy. While Chubb and Moe assert that democracy is to blame, Stone and colleagues argue that getting politics out of education is neither possible nor desirable: "America spent most of the twentieth century trying to take politics out of the schools. That was a mistake. . . . Successful educational reform ultimately requires a broad and sustainable coalition of support, and the route goes directly through, and not around politics."[22]

Politics is as central as markets are to successful application of educational reform in this country. It is as much a problem of civic capacity as it is of bureaucratic responsiveness. We want school personnel to be attentive to, and perhaps even scared by, their parent communities, but these school leaders must also have the political and economic resources with which they can achieve their visions of excellence in education. This is why we should care about democratic communities in education. Education is, at least partially, a public good, supported by people engaging in collective action, and it acts as a bastion against the inequalities caused by funding schools on the basis of the value of property values or the tuition payments that they can afford.

Making the Public Schools Better with Choice

Studies of school choice often examine the connection between parental choice and higher quality education as if there were a direct, causal relationship between choice and educational attainment. There is good reason for framing school choice in these straightforward terms. It is the policy question of ultimate concern for choice policy researchers. If we undertake this large experiment in facilitating competition in education, will we get better-educated students? The implicit assumption, however, is that there is a direct, at least potentially knowable, connection between the learning that takes place at the end of the line and the implementation of school choice policies.

It is a simple and powerful story. It is also a very important one. Given the low quality of educational services available in many districts, any evidence that school choice improves the education of those in the core urban areas would be most welcome. The connection between school choice and better student performance in this perspective is direct, a line of reasoning that makes the most sense when one thinks about choice from the point of view of students who enroll in choice programs, as no institutional change has to take place other than the choice program itself.

Of course there are still many other assumptions that one has to make to obtain benefits for the choice students. There must be a sufficient supply of better and affordable alternatives as well as adequate information about the quality of educational services in the choice options. Based on empirical research so far, there is no conclusive evidence that the introduction of school choice produces better educated students, as opposed to more satisfied parents, on which there is general agreement.[23] There have been some studies that found benefits for a subset of children participating in privately run voucher programs;[24] however, the two largest publicly funded voucher programs, in Cleveland and Milwaukee, have not shown any meaningful achievement gains for the participants.[25] School choice policies are quite new, and there remain very few programs that incorporate private schools. Researchers are still collecting data, so a lack of a research consensus is not surprising. It does not necessarily imply that choice schools will not eventually do a better job educating their students, only that the claim has not yet been adequately supported.

The deeper problem with focusing on the direct connection between school choice and student achievement is that—from the point of view of the students who remain behind in the public schools—it doesn't exist. For choice to improve the educational attainment of students in the public schools, the benefits of choice must work their way through a series of institutional changes. Public schools must become more responsive and competitive. The schools must change what they do, how they do it, and perhaps who does it. And any new practices or personnel that schools use to deliver these improved educational services must have some effect on what the students actually learn.

It is a long causal chain from parental choice to improving student performance in the existing public schools, from introducing school choice to improving the educational production at the end of the line. It consists mostly of entirely plausible, but poorly understood, relationships. However, the promise of better public schools with choice exerts a powerful effect on the educational reform debate nonetheless. At a minimum, there are three conditions that must be met in order for school choice to produce a meaningful change in student learning and achievement for those students who remain in the public schools. These connections result from thinking about school choice, not as an automatic trigger of better education, but as the introduction of market-based incentives to a preexisting public system of educational production.

There are many steps that might produce better public schools from choice, and it may make sense to think about these complex relationships in terms of three connections: the client connection, the organizational connection, and the classroom connection. The client connection requires that private school administrators be more responsive to their customers than are public school monopolists because of the power of consumers in the competitive environment of the marketplace.[26] Recall that Chubb and Moe faulted the lack of responsiveness on the part of public bureaucracies for leading to poorer educational services. The client connection is the first step in remediating the problems of direct democratic control on educational service delivery. Public school bureaucrats—under the threat of exit—get scared. The loss or potential loss of customers causes public school bureaucrats to pay more attention to their customers and less attention to procedures and superiors. Giving parents choices about where they send their children, and freeing them from the monopoly of the public schools, will force all schools to fundamentally change how they operate. They will become more consumer oriented, or they will go out of business. Those institutions that have inhibited educational innovation, including local school boards and state departments of education, will lose influence. Parents, as newly empowered consumers, will gain influence.

The second connection is an organizational one. It posits that the beneficial effects of increased bureaucratic responsiveness and customer attentiveness will translate into something different in what happens within individual schools. The organizational connection asserts that the structural changes produced by giving parents more choices will result in some meaningful change in what happens in the classroom or alternative classroom setting, in the educational services that are delivered, the personnel who deliver them, or the learning environment in which this all takes place. The third step, the classroom connection, asserts that these differences in educational services must have a meaningful effect on what students learn. In other words, what happens in the classroom or alternative learning space actually matters to student learning.

All three of these links are entirely plausible; however, none has been established with anything close to certainty. School choice has not been treated as a series of policy connections, so these questions have not, generally, been asked. The problem with multiple linkages of causality in the world of public policy is that the probabilities of something going wrong compound with each connection.[27]

My focus is on the first link in the causal chain, the client connection: the degree to which school choice produces a beneficial change in how public school bureaucrats respond to their community and their bureaucracies. The client connection asserts that the emergence of new forms of organizing public schools brought about by the introduction of market forces will force the public schools to become more aware of and responsive to their clients. My aim is to examine in detail this first link in the causal chain, both in terms of trying to find evidence for or against it and in terms of trying to figure out what it means for the public schools. As I hope will become evident, even this narrow slice of the school choice problem is quite complex and not at all as obvious as it may first appear.

These beneficial accountability effects are central to the assertion that school choice will induce beneficial bureaucratic changes on the public schools while it also encourages the development of institutional alternatives to them. In spite of its theoretical importance, relatively little attention has been paid to its study.[28] School choice policies, however ambitious, do little to change the delivery of educational services within the public schools other than to change the incentive structure under which the bureaucrats within schools operate. Choice policies involve—from the point of view of the existing public schools—little more than changes in the provision of incentives to public bureaucrats.

There are two potential counterarguments to the claim of better public schools under choice, and they must be kept separate in order to give choice policies a fair hearing. The first critique is that there may not be any efficiency gains from the introduction of choice. Public schools might not do anything in the presence of competition, particularly if there is no real threat that the public school bureaucrats will suffer any meaningful consequences. As yet, there is no empirical evidence that there are widespread efficiency gains from choice. Again, this does not mean that gains in efficiency might not eventually be realized. The second counterargument asserts that, while choice may lead to more responsive bureaucrats, there will be negative consequences in other areas that may or may not outweigh these bureaucratic efficiencies. In this book, I will consider both of these possibilities in some detail.

There is a lot riding on the prospect of school choice strengthening the client connection, especially for the kids in the remaining public schools. Unless one is willing to assert that school choice will produce an immediate, and effective, weeding out of poorly performing public schools and an equally effective replacement of those failing schools with new alternatives, then one must be concerned with the effects of choice on traditional public schools, at least in the short run. Of course, school choice advocates counter that bad public schools will close and will be replaced by more exciting alternatives. Although this is a reasonable argument, it moves the discussion from fixing poorly performing schools to closing them. It requires new decisions, like what to do with the kids in most poorly performing schools in the interim and what to do if the very best or even moderately good public or private schools do not want or cannot make room for choice students.

Any attempts to reform or improve the behaviors of public officials, including teachers and school principals, run into problems of agency. The term *agency* refers simply to the challenge of getting your person, your agent, to do what you want them to do or refrain from doing what you do not want them to do. Agency relationships are everywhere, from customers trying to get their cars fixed at a fair price to members of Congress keeping tabs on the behaviors of bureaucrats. The process is especially challenging if you cannot observe the behavior of your agent all the time or measure the quality of the work that they are doing with certitude. Both of these challenges are present in education.

These challenges are only magnified by the complexity of the relationships that are involved in the politics surrounding education. Political organizations are often described as a string of agency relationships.[29] In this agency string, somebody is trying to affect the behavior of or watch over someone else while being observed themselves. Public school principals, it seems, are more accurately described as operating within a web of agency relationships and within a system of common agency.[30] Public school principals are subject to the preferences of many actors, each with potentially diverging interests. Parents, teachers, voters, unions, school boards, and administrative superiors all have an interest in what happens in the public schools and may act as a brake on any gains in customer responsiveness on the part of the public schools.[31]

Bureaucratic responsiveness under school choice is a mediated thing. The decision of parents to exit when offered the choice interacts with the incentives under which school boards, teachers, unions, and state and district administrators operate. Many of these actors have levers to pull and might put pressure on school principals in the presence of customer exit. The pathways of control are numerous and interconnected, and they involve a variety of actors, including parents, interest groups, and state and local officials who may be elected or appointed. Simple agency models applied to public education may fail to capture meaningful aspects of control.

The placement of school principals at the center of a complicated web of agency relationships has several implications for how we think about the incentives under which public school principals operate. Some actors may be more powerful than others. Any efforts by one group to control the principals' actions may interact with the preferences of another group. The ways in which information flows through this agency web and is used by the various actors operating within it are relevant to what effect it has. Perhaps a school principal hears about a particular condition or decision from several of these actors, each with its own interests.

School choice directly affects only a subset of the relationships in this agency web: those connections that involve parents, who are now empowered to leave a given public school or, perhaps, the public schools entirely. Under choice, a subset of the parent community is allowed to exit from the agency web. This may affect how parents influence what the public school principals do. It may also affect the community of voters on which we rely to pressure the principals or school boards, to pass the school budget requests and vote for school board candidates, and otherwise to govern the educational process. Other actors may put pressure on school principals in the face of a mass exodus of clients, but these will be indirect effects, mediated by the choices parents themselves make.

What is most relevant, from the point of view of school choice, is the possibility that various school choice policies will differentially affect the provision of incentives for public school principals, by increasing or decreasing the leverage of any one of the key actors: parents, teachers, school boards, and administrators. The effects of policy reforms on public bureaucracies need to be understood in terms of common agency relationships, at least in those areas where public bureaucracies serve multiple constituencies.[32]

Thinking about educational control in a system in this way is most useful because it expands the idea of what it means for a public school to be responsive. School choice researchers often apply a very narrow definition of responsiveness, one that incorporates only the fulfillment of customer wishes on the part of public school bureaucrats. Defining responsiveness in this way ignores how schools are responsive to the larger democratic community and how public school leaders might nurture their parent communities to produce better educational services. It neglects the possibility that political participation involves much more than pressuring a bureaucracy: it includes a wide range of political activities.[33] Parents in the public schools are volunteers, voices of satisfaction and dissatisfaction, coproducers of learning, and voters in the electoral processes surrounding education.

Feedback Effects in Public Policy

As much as this book is about school choice, it is also a book about the dynamic effects of public policies on American democracy. As such, it lies within what is called the policy-feedback approach to the study of politics. The driving concern of policy-feedback researchers is how policies, once enacted, shape the political behaviors of citizens who, in turn, shape future policies.[34] There is an increasing consensus in this literature that policies can and do have measurable effects on the functioning of democracy. We know this: Policies matter to politics. They change the future political participation of those targeted by the policies, shaping citizens' attitudes toward politics, citizens' conceptions of themselves as political actors, and how individuals allocate and devote their political resources and mobilize around political causes.[35] Scholars have observed these relationships in the connections between the enactment of the GI Bill and the civic-mindedness of an entire generation of veterans[36] and the implementation of Social Security policy and the creation of a large, effective coalition of seniors, rich and poor alike.[37]

The policy-feedback approach owes much to the historical institutionalist school of political development in states and societies. The key insight of this framework is that policies shape and reshape political coalitions.[38] Rather than take the implementation of public policies as the endpoint of research, scholars within this approach argue that enactment and implementation change the future direction of policies and the set of future policies that do or do not get enacted.

In the view of those operating in the historical institutionalist approach, government is not an unwanted by-product of development but a necessary tool for securing political equality. In *Diminished Democracy,* Theda Skocpol takes on the currently popular assertion that government is inimical to civic involvement and needs to be replaced with policies that pander to individualistic concerns. Skocpol bases her critique on the critical role that government, especially national government, plays in securing resources for poorer citizens. What we now recognize as modern American civic life, according to Skocpol, was created and nourished through mass mobilization and robust national governmental action.

Central to this endeavor is the creation of cross-class coalitions through "flourishing membership federations" that bridge the gaps between citizens of different social and economic strata.[39] The national PTA, for example, brought parents of different classes together in a shared enterprise in a way that more narrow school-based parent-teacher organizations and booster clubs do not, though they are effective in bonding people together in these homogenous, class-based school communities.[40] While a capacious governmental authority has been portrayed as the root problem in education, Skocpol reminds us that "effective democracy requires powerful representative government and strong, encompassing associations that afford collective leverage by and for the majority."[41]

Policy-feedback researchers have built on the historical institutionalist research by adding a focus on the ways policies change political behaviors, especially of mass publics, and the ways that policies restructure the set of incentives under which individuals do or do not engage in politics. Policies—themselves the result of political choices and processes—determine future political outcomes by virtue of the ways that policies influence and constrain individual behaviors. It is because of this dynamic that scholars operating in the tradition typically refer to policy-feedback loops.

In her study of Social Security in the United States, Andrea Louise Campbell finds that the structure of Social Security policy has created a politically involved, cross-class coalition of seniors that has, in turn, secured considerable funding for the program in spite of competing demands on the federal budget. Senior Americans are disproportionately active, and poorer seniors even more so. This has come about because of the design of the program. It is universal, open to all seniors, and there is no shame in participating in it. Campbell's work lies firmly within the policy-feedback approach in that it explores how policies shape the citizens who, in turn, shape the policies of the future: "Policy begets participation begets policy in a cycle that results not in equal protection of interests, but in outcomes biased toward the politically active. Thus the very quality of democratic government is shaped by the kinds of policies it pursues."[42]

Campbell also warns against attempts at privatizing Social Security, because they are likely to reverse these gains in bridging gaps between seniors of different classes and binding them together in an effective political voice. While we cannot yet observe the potentially destructive changes brought about by privatizing social security, since we have not done so yet, I can, and do, find evidence of the same kinds of processes in the area of education. Private markets beget privatized political choices.

Though the central ideas of policy-feedback researchers are not new, merging the idea that policies shape citizens with empirical methods and a focus on incentives has created a new and exciting research agenda in the study of policies, politics, and democracy. The policy-feedback approach has the potential to bridge the gap between those who argue that we need to consider social and political outcomes as the result of the actions of small, rational, autonomous individuals and those who argue that the only real traction one can gain on studying political outcomes is by broadening our focus to the dynamic aspects of social relationships in the world of public policy.

Much, however, remains to be done. Scholars are unanimous in the conclusion that we need to know more about the details and mechanisms of policy-feedback loops.[43] My work here explores the mechanisms through which a certain type of policy—the facilitation of competition—affects both the distribution and the character of political participation in the realm of education. In addition, most of the policy-feedback studies have been done on policies that were implemented some time ago, where political possibilities have long since been opened or closed for the future. Examining school choice policy allows me to look for and evaluate policy-feedback effects before it is too late to do anything about them. Finally, not enough work has been done on the connection between the contexts in which policies are implemented—especially community resources—and how the policy-feedback loops play out.[44] The potential consequences of school choice on resource-rich and resource-poor communities place this question front and center in my analyses and is itself only one example of the redefinition of citizenship and the public sphere currently under way in the United States.[45]

Progression of the Argument

Though a great deal has been written about school choice in the past few years, I believe that several factors set this book apart from much of the work in this field. In taking up the issue of the effects of choice on the customer orientation of the public schools, my hope is to broaden our understanding of what it means for a public bureaucracy to be responsive to its customers while also dependent upon its citizens for support and oversight. I treat public school principals as strategic actors hoping to make the most efficient use of their parent communities in a way that includes the community-building aspects of that responsiveness.

By locating the effects of school choice on the behaviors of citizens and consumers in a larger debate about the role of markets and politics in sustaining democratic communities, I hope to make a small contribution toward a deeper understanding of both the likely consequences of school choice policies and of the connection between democratic participation, resource inequalities, and marketplace reforms. Finally, by employing both qualitative and quantitative analysis in a study of the relationship between citizens, consumers, and the schools, I hope to offer a depth of analysis necessary to a careful exploration of these important relationships.

I must warn readers, however, that I am going to take them on a rather complicated journey and implore them to bear with me a bit. Granted, my various sources of data are (charitably) eclectic and (less charitably) cobbled together.[46] However, examining the effects of marketplace reforms on citizens and institutions involves multiple contexts and diverse methods. It requires examining data from different programs and locations, because there is not yet a "super-choice" program that incorporates both public and private choice, has been around long enough to observe on-the-ground changes, and involves sufficiently large numbers of students and schools to study systematically. I raise many more empirical questions than I settle. My goal is not to put to rest narrow debates of concern to a small group of researchers but to thoughtfully and thoroughly examine the connection between big questions in democratic politics and public policies on the ground. I leave the task of achieving a final resolution of many of these debates to other researchers.

I am going to focus on two of the most talked-about school choice programs: the provision of vouchers to attend private schools and the creation of charter schools. The first facilitates exit to the private sector, and second facilitates exit within the public space. I will spend most of my time on charter schools, examining them using different methods in two states and arguing that the dynamics of introducing marketlike reforms within public education are more complex, interesting, and hopeful than those that facilitate exit from the public space, primarily because the customers, and any new skills they are learning and developing from participation in the choice program, are retained within the public school system.

In chapter 2, I begin with school choice policies that facilitate exit to the private sector, taking the specific case of the Milwaukee voucher program. The first piece of the puzzle to unravel is the relationship between a parent's decision to exit to a private school and their political participation, within and beyond the school walls. I examine voucher programs in the context of the effects of exit on the participatory behaviors of the parents who choose to participate. I consider the dual possibilities that more active parents may be more likely to exit when offered the chance and that these same parent-choosers may become more effective in their political participation as a result of their exercise of the power to choose. I consider the implications for the expression of voice within the public schools that have been left behind.

I conclude the chapter by considering the role of institutional design and context in the relationship between school choice and parental involvement. I use data from a national survey of parents to examine the comparative democratic consequences of exit within and beyond the public schools. In addition, I take up the as-yet-overlooked issue of how the consequences of exit on the expression of parental political participation might be different for resource-rich and resource-poor communities, raising the possibility that that there may be significant differences in outcomes based on the preexisting stock of political and economic resources within a school community.

In chapter 3, and for the rest of the analyses of the book, I turn to the question of charter schools, which offer many potential advantages over private voucher programs, by virtue of the fact that any skimming and cultivation of parental political participation will occur within the larger system of public support for and control over public education in the United States. In addition, I move beyond data that others have collected, employing original qualitative and quantitative analyses for the rest of the book. Chapter 3 explores the results of observational studies that I conducted of public school principals in New Jersey encountering choice within their districts. I use these observational data to unpack parental involvement in education, realizing that parental participation refers itself to a complex group of behaviors and interactions. Understanding the different types of parental involvement is crucial to extending the discussion beyond simply joining a parent-teacher association.

In chapter 4, I turn to Minnesota, using a survey of charter school principals, traditional public school principals facing charter schools in their districts, and traditional public school principals not facing charter schools to explore the effects of charter schools on bureaucratic responsiveness and attempts by these school leaders to reach out to and incorporate their parent communities in meaningful areas of school policy. I examine the extent to which charter schools result in a more customer-focused principalship, increased efforts to incorporate parents into school policy decisions on the part of these public school leaders, and the effects of these efforts on the actual participation within the schools by parents as a result of charter school reforms. This is the possibility for bureaucratic regeneration asserted, but not yet proven, by school choice advocates.

Chapter 5 extends the discussion of charter schools and parental involvement in public education beyond the walls of the school, to incorporate the effects of charter schools on participation in school budget referenda. I return to New Jersey, to look at voter turnout and the results of school budget referenda in charter school and non–charter school districts. This is the (also unproven) assertion of democratic degeneration made by those who are worried about the experiments that we are currently undertaking.

Chapter 6 revisits what I have learned from these analyses about the larger bureaucratic and democratic consequences of school choice in the United States. In addition, I take what I have learned about customer responsiveness in public education to offer some suggestions for policymakers struggling to achieve an educational vision that makes room for both liberty and equality.

Taken together, these results paint a robust and understandable picture of what effects we can expect to see when we bring marketlike forces to the provision of public education, particularly how those effects are going to be structured and determined by the nature of the choice program itself. The two most currently discussed school choice reforms—providing parents vouchers to send their kids to private schools and the establishment of charter schools—are much more different than they are similar.

The effects on the deliberative processes involved with educational governance by privatizing the political behavior of those who participate, or do not participate, in the institutions and processes of educational governance are themselves institutionally determined. Public and private choice options have very different systemic consequences. Private choice options deprive public educational communities of their most valuable resources. Public choice options empower customers and retain them within the public system. In the absence of any demonstrable effects on academic achievement brought about by subsidizing exit to the private sector through the provision of vouchers, I argue that policymakers should turn an especially critical eye to their implementation. In the case of charter schools, we should, of course, expect and hope to see achievement gains as well. However, the costs to the public school system are lower for charters than for vouchers and indicate a different critical standard in evaluating their effects on achievement.

Robert Dahl asks if there is an "inescapable trade-off" between the expression of individual liberty and the protection of democratic equality.[47] My answer is that there is something inescapable about the relationship between equality and liberty, markets and politics in education, but that it is something other than a trade-off. Markets and politics can affect, and damage, each other. The privileging of adversarial processes in education through choice policies can both benefit parents by creating more responsive schools and also, in the process, damage the collective efforts aimed at governing and supporting the public schools, depending on if they are public or private.

It appears that Chubb and Moe are correct, but incompletely. The institutions of direct democratic control may very well have deleterious effects on educational production. Weakening these institutions can make for more responsive schools, if one defines responsiveness using a narrow, customer-firm framework. Market forces can be useful to correct the ills of politics; however, these corrections produce their own consequences in the political space that they target, particularly if one looks beyond the immediate control over schools by customers and locates these relationships within a larger democratic community.

The findings presented in this book challenge the prospect of market forces fixing public education in the United States, uniformly and unequivocally, and without consideration of which sector—public or private—benefits from these democratic and bureaucratic consequences. This is not because market forces are ineffective, but because they are applied within an institutional framework that relies upon a democratic community that is itself transformed by these reforms. There may be efficiency costs to be paid as the price for democratic control. However, these costs may be worth paying, to preserve the collective endeavor of public education in the face of the atomizing tendencies of private markets.

Part of the allure of school choice is the assertion that choice will make all schools, even the public schools, better, by forcing them to adapt to the marketplace or perish in their disconnectedness. This assertion allows school choice advocates to have it both ways: Parents will reject poorly performing public schools in numbers, but the kids left behind will benefit as well, since the bureaucrats in these schools will strive to improve services in the presence of this new exit option. The results presented in this book challenge this assertion and show that an uncritical faith in the markets can have a devastating impact on the democratic communities in which these market forces are unleashed.

2 | Leaving the Public Schools Behind

> Suppose at some point, for whatever reason, the public
> schools deteriorate. Thereupon, increasing numbers of qual-
> ity-education-conscious parents will send their children to
> private schools. This "exit" may occasion some impulse
> toward an improvement of the public schools: but here again
> this impulse is far less significant than the loss to the public
> schools of those member-customers who would be most moti-
> vated and determined to put up a fight against the deteriora-
> tion if they did not have the alternative of the private schools.
>
> —*Albert Hirschman,* Exit, Voice, and Loyalty[1]

IN THE BEGINNING, school choice was mostly about race. In spite of the
justifications of choice on efficiency grounds made by Milton Friedman,
early school choice policies were designed either to perpetuate racial segregation or to try to overcome it. In the case of providing parents with
public funds to send their children to private schools, it was a case of
Southern school districts and state legislatures attempting to subvert the
U.S. Supreme Court in its efforts to desegregate the public schools. In Vir-
ginia, for example, the Prince Edward County Board of Supervisors
refused in 1959 to fund its public schools. Instead, a private foundation
was set up to provide white children with state- and county-funded tuition
grants to attend private schools. The Supreme Court of the United States
overturned this early voucher program, instead voicing its impatience with
such shenanigans.[2]

Today, however, private voucher programs are usually targeted at
inner city school districts and are presented as options for parents of color,
given serious issues with the academic quality of the city public schools.
Vouchers work like tickets paid for by the state, redeemable for tuition at
participating schools, including private religious and nonreligious ones. It
is important to note that voucher programs need not exclude public
schools from the choice mix. In fact, one of the original publicly funded
voucher programs—the Ohio Pilot Scholarship Program—allowed public
schools in fifteen neighboring school districts to accept the vouchers of

Cleveland's public school students. No public schools in these wealthier districts with smaller minority student populations chose to accept vouchers. School officials argued that the vouchers—and extra offers of tuition money from the state—were insufficient reimbursement for the costs involved.[3] The result of the exclusion of suburban public and private schools—whether by choice or a poor incentive structure—is that vouchers are an inner city thing, unlikely to offer much hope of ending the economic isolation of inner city children.[4]

In the case of early efforts at establishing school choice within a public system, the goal was to try to reverse—or at least stem—the flight of white middle-class parents to suburban school systems. The tool for this ambitious goal was the magnet school, a public school designed around a particular theme, such as science or the arts, that parents could choose instead of their assigned neighborhood school. Magnet schools are still around, and the very best are as good as any school, public or private. In general, however, they have not produced racial integration or stemmed the recent trend toward resegregation in public education.

My point is not to claim that private or public choice programs are necessarily going to exacerbate or improve racial segregation in the United States, but to point out that social, racial, ethnic, and economic contexts have always been closely connected to providing choices in education and will likely continue to do so in the future. School choice policies are going to be superimposed on real communities, whose characteristics may, in part, determine the beneficial and destructive outcomes for those communities. In addition, specific choice policies are very different from each other, in their histories, legacies, and potential for beneficial or destructive repercussions.

Few debates in education policy today are as controversial as the question of whether students who enroll in private schools with the aid of publicly funded vouchers are better off for it. Studies of the original two public voucher programs, in Cleveland and Milwaukee, found insufficient evidence to determine that voucher programs were having any beneficial effects for their enrollees.[5] The strongest statement in support of vouchers comes from a study of a privately funded voucher program in New York City.[6] The authors of the study concluded that African American children demonstrated significant achievement gains compared to program applicants who were rejected by lottery. The fact that selection was by lottery is useful, as one doesn't have to worry so much about whether differences in academic achievement might be due to the characteristics of parents or students.

The evidence from New York, however, has come under considerable scrutiny by Alan Krueger and Pei Zhu. In the original study, students whose fathers but not mothers were African American were excluded from the analysis. When Krueger and Zhu reclassified these students, however, most of the achievement gains disappeared. Though the argument hinges on a somewhat technical point, it highlights just how little evidence there is, and how cautious all readers of such studies should be.[7] In short, vouchers have yet to prove their worth. Given the uncertainty surrounding the achievement benefits of vouchers, it seems worthwhile to expand the frame of analysis beyond the test-score effects of voucher recipients and to examine the effects of these programs on the larger institutional and social contexts in which they are implemented.

Political Activism and the Consequences of Exit

In the previous chapter, I argued that parents need to be thought of as resources, not only for their students but for the schools with which they interact. We know very little about how shifting a small group of parents out of the public schools and into private schools will affect either the schools that they enter or the ones that they leave. In this chapter, I begin the empirical analyses of the book by looking at the political consequences of policies that facilitate exit to the private sector on parental involvement with their newly chosen private schools. I will consider two contrasting, but not necessarily incompatible, possibilities for the effects of private-school voucher programs on parental involvement in education. Each of these arguments has its advocates in the school choice debate. The first is the concern that voucher programs will skim the most capable and involved parents from the public schools and into the private schools. This is the privatization of voice hypothesis, based on Albert Hirschman's concepts of exit and voice. Active choosers will self-select out of their assigned public schools according to their political effectiveness and involvement, and the aggregation of these choices will lead to a redistribution of resources of political control and advocacy away from the public schools and toward the private options.

The privatization of voice hypothesis is closely connected to critiques of school choice based on the potential of cream-skimming. The traditional skimming argument warns that wealthier parents and more talented students will be more likely to enroll in choice options, thereby increasing educational stratification by race, class, and ability. There is increasing empirical evidence that active choosers in public and private choice systems are better educated and better off than people who do not participate in choice programs.[8]

An important theme in studies of school choice and parents is that a subset of parents is well informed and exerts a disproportionate effect on the production of services in that marketplace. This group of parents acts to ensure that the educational marketplace responds to the wishes of parents in spite of the informational challenges that the majority of less activist parents face.[9] Although the authors of one study found evidence that the competitive pressures exerted by marginal customers benefited all, activism was not independent from identity and economics. Among parents who chose their child's school, 31 percent were college educated, while only 11 percent of nonchoosers were similarly educated. Related studies that focused on how parents gather information about schools when given choices found that the quality of informational networks in education was also heterogeneously distributed.[10] More educated, wealthier, and majority-ethnicity parents were more likely to employ informal and more effective sources of information, rather than relying on officially defined and controlled sources, confirming, in the realm of school choice, that political voice is biased toward the wealthy and educated.[11]

These findings are most problematic when one considers that the same marginal consumers may be the first to leave when offered choice options, which raises questions about the effects their departure may have for the institutional control of public schools left behind. Not all parents are equal in the exchange between parents and principals. Some parents are well-connected to other well-connected parents. These parents may have more effective voices to devote to watching over the school or more resources to help the principal achieve his or her vision. These parents are the ones who make the first calls in the classroom phone-tree. Well-connected parents can offer school principals links to other key members of the network, which gives these active parents more leverage over the principals' behavior than they might otherwise have. This may be why principals listen to activist parents, even if their management requires the investment of nontrivial amounts of time and effort. It may also suggest why it matters to the performance of the public schools if these well-connected parents leave for private school choice options.

Advocates of choice programs counter the significance, but not the accuracy, of concerns about parental skimming on two fronts. First, in conceding potential negative effects of parental skimming, advocates argue that choice programs should be, and are, targeted at minority and lower-income families. Moreover, they assert, the question is not whether skimming will take place, but whether the segregation that will take place will be worse than the considerable segregation under the current system.[12] This is a much more powerful counterargument, given the serious inequities under the current system.

However, this counterargument does not address the organizational implications of skimming when exit from the public sector is facilitated or subsidized. If the introduction of school choice causes the most active voices to go private, then the public options might become less constrained by, and less responsive to, parental interests over time. While choice may initially cause public school principals to be more attentive to parental wishes, over time the lowest quality schools may end up with the least involved parents. The most difficult schools, therefore, might become even more difficult to change and improve. This possibility becomes potentially more problematic as one considers the expansion of voucher programs to include much larger populations.

The second theory that I will examine builds on social capital research to assert that active choosers increase their political effectiveness as a result of the choices they have made, raising the overall ability for parents to control their schools.[13] Rather than be worried by the possibility of parental skimming, these scholars argue, we should be encouraged by the possibility that choosing schools will make parents more active. Parents who are able to leave their assigned schools and choose one that they feel is better for their child will take a larger, more assertive role in their child's new school.[14]

Institutional arrangements that facilitate private choices in education, according to this argument, increase parental involvement in the political processes surrounding schooling and make these parents better citizens, thereby increasing social capital in the community. The definition of social capital that the proponents of this view use is relational, existing not within individuals but in the networked connections between them.[15] Social capital helps individuals overcome problems of collective action through participation in social networks, built on trust, and in acceptance of a set of norms. Social capital is, therefore, important to the proper functioning of a democratic society.[16] Choice, therefore, is likely to have beneficial social consequences for all parents, even those who are not involved in the program but who benefit from the effects of increased participatory skills brought about through the exercise of those choices.[17]

Two questions arise from thinking about activist parents in relation to policies that facilitate exit to the private sector or within the public sector: What happens to the public schools that these parents leave? And what happens to the parents as a consequence of their participation in the program and the exit that it facilitates? I examine both issues, one based on the skimming of activist parents from the public schools as a consequence of the voucher programs and the other on the beneficial effects of the exercise of choice.

Parental Skimming in the Milwaukee Voucher Program

The Milwaukee school choice program, enacted in 1990, provides a payment from public funds to parents of students in the Milwaukee public schools (MPS) to send their children to private schools in Milwaukee, provided those families meet certain requirements.[18] Religious and nonreligious schools in Milwaukee may choose to participate in the program. The program remains small, and more parents apply than receive the vouchers. No more than a percent and a half of MPS parents were allowed to participate as of the 1994–95 school year, the last year in which systematic data were collected.

Most of the empirical work on the Milwaukee voucher program has been conducted by John Witte in an analysis of parent surveys associated with the Milwaukee school choice program.[19] Surveys were mailed in the fall and spring of each school year to all applicants to the Milwaukee choice program for the 1990–91 school year and each year following.[20] Attempts were also made to survey both choice-accepted and choice-rejected parents. In addition, a similar survey was mailed to a random sample of MPS parents in the spring of 1991,[21] allowing comparisons of the participation of choosers and "typical" public school parents.

In his analysis, Witte compares the self-reports of school involvement of parents who applied for the choice program with the random sample of MPS parents. He finds that parents who applied to the Milwaukee voucher program were more likely to be involved with the child's education, more likely to contact their school, and more likely to be involved in parent-teacher association (PTA) activities than the MPS parents. Witte connects these findings to Hirschman's concepts of exit and voice, observing that this self-selection may deprive the public schools of their most active voices.[22] In addition, he finds that those who were accepted into the choice program displayed higher participation in the spring of their acceptance year.

While Witte's results suggest a process of participatory skimming, they are not sufficient to establish its existence. The conclusions are all based on bivariate models that do not control for possible correlates of participation, notably parental income and education. In addition, they do not examine the changes in participation over time—to see if other social capital–building processes might also be at work—nor do they speak to the crucial issue of differences in patterns of participation among different subgroups of the Milwaukee choice program participants, to see if the processes of social capital formation unleashed by the Milwaukee voucher program depend at all on the characteristics of the members of that community. Therefore, while the analyses in this chapter are based on data that have already been collected and analyzed, my hope is that they provide a first-order contribution to the understanding of key issues involved but often ignored in the school choice debate.

The goal of the first empirical analysis of this chapter is to compare the self-reported levels of school involvement of parents who apply for the choice program with the random sample of MPS parents taken in the same school year. This helps us assess whether there was any skimming of more active parents with the introduction of the Milwaukee voucher program, while controlling for possible correlates of political involvement, especially parental education and income.

Parents were asked in the survey whether they had been a member of a parent-teacher organization, whether they had attended a parent-teacher association meeting, and whether they had taken part in activities of PTAs during the past year. In my models, parents were given one point for responding "yes" to each these questions, resulting in three dichotomous school participation measures.[23] I also constructed a summary PTA participation variable by giving one point to each parent for each "yes," for a maximum of three points.[24] I used these responses to construct regression models of parental involvement in PTAs in a way that controls for other factors that might influence a parent's involvement in his or her school's PTA, such as the parent's minority group status, primary use of a language other than English, household income, parental education, frequency of contact by the child's school encouraging parental participation, and whether or not the parent had applied for the choice program for the 1990–91 school year, the first year of the program.[25] Table 2.1 presents the results of these school participation models.

The results in table 2.1 allow me to examine if parents who applied to the Milwaukee voucher program were different from the random sample of Milwaukee public school parents in their membership in the PTA (column 1), in their attendance at PTA meetings (column 2), in participation in PTA activities (column 3), and in a summary variable composed of all three of these behaviors (column 4)—controlling for other things that might affect a parent's likelihood of getting involved. A significant and positive estimate on the key variable—having applied for the choice program—therefore would indicate that participatory skimming is occurring, as the program is drawing an active subset of Milwaukee parents.

It is clear from the Milwaukee results that more active parents are signing up for the voucher program. While choice program applicants do not appear more likely to belong to a parent teacher organization than the

TABLE 2.1.   PTA Participation in Milwaukee: Choosers versus Random
Milwaukee Public Schools Sample

	Belong to PTA (0–1) (1)	Attend Meetings (0–1) (2)	Actively Participate (0–1) (3)	Total PTA Score (0–3) (4)
Parent applied for choice program in 1990	–0.01 (0.12)	0.38*** (0.11)	0.33*** (0.11)	0.27*** (0.09)
Student is member of minority group	–0.003 (0.09)	0.25*** (0.08)	–0.09 (0.08)	0.08 (0.07)
Parent's primary language other than English	0.24 (0.28)	0.49** (0.21)	0.17 (0.24)	0.32 (0.20)
Household income	0.10*** (0.02)	0.02 (0.02)	0.03* (0.02)	0.05*** (0.01)
Parental education	0.11*** (0.03)	0.03 (0.02)	0.14*** (0.03)	0.11*** (0.02)
School to parent contact about fund-raising and volunteering	0.51*** (0.05)	0.51*** (0.11)	0.64*** (0.05)	0.62*** (0.04)
N	1,519	1,519	1,519	1,519
Constant	–2.23*** (0.17)	–0.91*** (0.13)	–1.46*** (0.14)	—
Cut points	—	—	—	1.00 (0.12) 1.81 (0.12) 2.44 (0.13)
Wald chi^2(6)	179.23	49.21	224.15	311.6
Prob > chi^2	0.00	0.00	0.00	0.00

Source: Data from Witte and Thorn 1995.

Note: Columns 1 through 3 present probit regression results. Column 4 presents ordered probit regression results. Standard error estimates are in parentheses. The dependent variable in columns 1 through 3 is coded as 0 if the parent did not belong to the PTA, attend meetings, or actively participate in the PTA, 1 if the parent did. The dependent variable in column 4 is coded from 0 to 3, with parents receiving 1 point for each of the three participatory activities. Positive coefficient estimates are associated with a higher probability of participating, controlling for other predictors.

*$p < 0.1$;   **$p < .05$;   ***$p < .01$, two-tailed.

random sample, they appear to be significantly more likely to have attended PTA meetings and to have participated in PTA activities than a random sample of Milwaukee parents in the year prior to signing up for the voucher lottery. It appears that a skimming of active parents is occurring in Milwaukee, at least as it relates to PTA activities.

There are also some other interesting, and intuitively coherent, findings in the data. In general, there does not appear to be a clear connection between racial and ethnic status or language use and the likelihood of participating in the PTA, other than attendance at PTA meetings. This is not surprising, as the program is targeted at lower-income parents and is implemented within a central city with a high minority student population. We cannot be sure, however, that larger-scale voucher programs will not lead to racial, ethnic, or income stratification.

Higher-income and more highly educated parents are more likely to belong to and participate in their parent-teacher associations. These patterns of participation are well established and consistent with the literature on political activity.[26] Finally, participation is positively associated with efforts made by schools to encourage voluntarism among their parent communities. This is important and encouraging for any choice program, public or private. If schools that face a system of choice do make an effort to get their customers involved, then these results suggest that a school's efforts will be rewarded with greater parental participation.

It is possible to convert these somewhat difficult to interpret regression coefficient estimates into probabilities in order to more fully explore the degree to which choice program applicants displayed higher levels of participation than the random sample of public school parents using a simulation-based approach to interpreting regression results.[27] Table 2.2 presents the predicted probabilities of school involvement obtained using these stochastic simulation methods, along with the estimated standard errors and confidence intervals drawn around the predicted values.

A confidence interval may be thought of as a band of uncertainty around a value, which allows one to account for the uncertainty inherent in sampling only a portion of the target population. When the confidence intervals associated with the values for a particular variable do not overlap between two different comparison groups, then one can conclude with more confidence that the values reported really do differ statistically between the two groups in question. The results of table 2.2, therefore, allow me to make predictions on the probability of a parent belonging to, attending the meetings of, or being involved in the activities of the PTA, depending on whether they applied for the Milwaukee choice program or not (while controlling for other variables in a way that incorporates the stochastic nature of making these kinds of predictions).

While the probability of formal membership in the PTA does not appear to vary between choosers and the control group, the probabilities of attending PTA meetings and taking part in activities of these organizations are significantly higher for applicants to the choice program than for the random MPS parent sample.[28] Moreover, the confidence intervals drawn around the probabilities derived from meetings and activities coefficient estimates do not overlap, indicating greater confidence that these estimated probabilities are significantly higher for choosers than for

TABLE 2.2.   Probabilities of Participating: Choosers versus Random
Milwaukee Public Schools Sample

	Mean (1)	Standard Error (2)	95% Confidence Interval (3)
Belonging to PTA			
Choosers	0.18	(0.03)	[0.12–0.24]
Milwaukee Public Schools sample	0.18	(0.01)	[0.16–0.20]
Going to PTA meetings			
Choosers	0.51	(0.04)	[0.42–0.58]
Milwaukee Public Schools sample	0.36	(0.01)	[0.33–0.38]
Being active in PTA			
Choosers	0.48	(0.04)	[0.39–0.56]
Milwaukee Public Schools sample	0.35	(0.01)	[0.32–0.38]
N	1,519		

Source: Data from Witte and Thorn 1995.
Note: Probabilities obtained using Clarify (see King, Tomz, and Wittenberg 2000).

the peer group from which they self-selected. The Milwaukee voucher program appears to be drawing parents who are much more likely to be
involved in the PTA than those parents who remain behind in the public
system.[29]

By targeting school choice programs at low-income and minority communities, it may be possible to avoid skimming based on race, ethnicity,
and socioeconomic status. However, these targeted choice programs will
drain the most active and involved parents from the public schools and
divert their participatory resources to the private sector. This may be a
problem both on equity grounds—in that it unfairly drains the public
schools—but, most important, it is a problem for the market-based theory
of public school reform. It seems much more tenuous to assert that active
customers will put pressure on the public schools to improve if those customers have already left for the private sector.

Social Capital Formation and Vouchers

In order to look for the dynamic effects of participation in the voucher
program on the behaviors of parents brought about by social
capital–building processes, I use a different, but related set of data from
the Milwaukee public choice program. Each spring of the program, sur-

veys were sent to all applicants—accepted as well as rejected—asking them the same set of questions about their participation in their child's school during the previous year (in the fall survey) as during the current year (during the spring survey). This allows me to look for year-over-year changes in parental participation. My goal is to compare accepted and rejected parents on these year-over-year changes, to look for evidence that participation in the voucher program is encouraging parents to become more participatory.

That acceptance into the program was made by lottery offers particular advantages for my analysis, as it is possible to isolate changes in participation that arise from participation in the voucher program from parental characteristics. The challenge, however, is that not all applicants were reached in the spring wave of the survey. In fact, only 48 percent of parents surveyed in the fall of a given year were reinterviewed in the spring. This raises the issue of sample attrition: my analyses could lead to biased conclusions, since those parents who were not reachable in the second wave might display different patterns of participation from those who were. I can never really be sure that they did not.

It is, therefore, important to compare the groups of parents who were later reinterviewed with those who dropped out, to look for causes or signs of attrition bias. I present the mean scores and confidence intervals of key variables in detail in appendix A; however, given the importance of the issue, I will discuss the patterns that I observed. As one might expect, parents who were rejected were less likely to be reinterviewed in the following spring than those parents who were accepted. Rejected parents constituted 28 percent of the fall survey sample—which was taken at the time of application—but 49 percent of the spring sample. This may be a cause for concern, since the randomization process that decided whether a parent was accepted may be compromised by the nonrandom processes of whether that parent decided to participate in the spring interview round.

There are some small differences between those parents who were reinterviewed and those who were not; however, these differences might work against finding gains in participation in the combined groups, since for those parents, all else being equal, year-over-year gains in participation would be less likely given higher initial participation scores. It is encouraging to note that both sets of parents report generally similar levels of participation in the previous year. In addition, the only sizable difference between the two sets of parents is in household income. Parents in the attrition sample displayed higher incomes than those who were reinterviewed. This might work against finding gains in participation for rejected parents, since income and participation are positively correlated.

Comparing possible attrition in the samples of parents who were accepted or rejected from the program raises a few cautions, but it does not indicate that attrition will dominate my subsequent findings. Though there do appear to be small differences in the baseline scores of my accepted and rejected parent populations, some would work for or against finding relative gains in participation for the voucher-accepted and -rejected populations, and the confidence intervals suggest that I cannot reject the hypothesis that these differences are due only to the uncertainties inherent in sampling.

Choice-accepted parents report higher fall participation than choice-rejected parents on belonging to the PTA, lower baseline scores for attendance at meetings, and higher scores on the summary measure. In addition, the choice-rejected population displays higher scores on both parental income and education, both of which are recognized to tend to increase participation. This suggests that any bias introduced by attrition would either work against or have no effect on year-over-year gains in participation. It is, of course, impossible to know for sure whether underlying attitudes might result in different changes in participation; the expectation is that any differences would work against finding gains in either group, and readers should be cautioned by any biases that might result from these differences.[30]

Having discussed the possibilities of attrition bias, I now turn to the findings associated with my social capital models. According to the social capital hypothesis, one would expect that involvement in the voucher program would lead to increased participation on the part of participants. While the data in this analysis were collected from surveys of the same program, the focus is slightly different. Here, the dependent variable is constructed from subtracting the fall reports of PTA involvement from the spring report for the same parents in the first year following their acceptance to or rejection from the program. Based on these two reports, I create a new variable with a range from one to negative one indicating whether a parent has become more involved, experienced no change in involvement, or become less involved, according to the same PTA participation measures as before. A parent who did not change his or her PTA membership, attendance at meetings, or activity in the PTA over the course of the year would receive a zero on that measure.[31]

These changes in participation, along with a change in the same summary measure of PTA participation, are treated as a function of household income and parental education as before, along with indicator variables capturing the year in which the parent first applied to the choice program, to capture any effects of the "first responders" to these programs. In addition, I constructed a variable representing the difference in frequency of contact between school and parent about volunteering. Positive estimates on this frequency change variable indicate that the parent feels that whatever school his or her child is in this year is doing more contacting about volunteerism than last year's school. This is important because many private schools require or strongly suggest parental involvement as part of their policies. The lack of a variable indicating a specific contact for PTA participation within private schools might prevent me from fully capturing the role of the schools in creating social capital.

Though the contact change variable may not completely control for private school outreach efforts, its inclusion does add some confidence to the assertion that any gains in participation shown by program participants were at least partly due to the fact of their participation and not entirely due to the school's efforts, though it very well may be that both factors are at work.[32] Table 2.3 presents the regression results of these changes in the participation models. Positive coefficient estimates on the key independent variable—acceptance into the choice program—provide evidence on social capital–building effects in the program participants, at least as it relates to this admittedly narrow set of participation measures.

Evidence from the Milwaukee voucher program strongly suggests that parents who are accepted into the voucher program demonstrate greater gains in participation than those parents who were not accepted into the program, even when controlling for other variables. Coefficient estimates on all three participation variables and the summary variable are significant and positive.[33] There is also some evidence that the participatory gains for parents in the voucher program are linked to the socioeconomic status of the parent.

It appears that more educated parents within the targeted population benefit more than their less educated counterparts, in spite of the fact that this program is targeted at low-income parents (though this result is not uniformly significant). While one may not see stratification by income between choice participants and nonparticipants, there is evidence that there will be a stratification of benefit among choice participants by the level of parental education. That the change in contact frequency variables are all positive and significant supports the idea that schools can play a meaningful role in encouraging parental participation among their parents (chap. 4).

Simulation techniques can be used again to create and draw confidence intervals around the underlying probabilities of the regressions. In this

TABLE 2.3.   One-Year Changes in Participation: Choice Accepted versus Rejected in Milwaukee

	Change in Belonging (–1 to 1) (1)	Change in Attendance (–1 to 1) (2)	Change in Activity (–1 to 1) (3)	Total PTA Change (–3 to 3) (4)
Parent accepted in the	0.33**	0.45***	0.51***	0.62***
program	(0.15)	(0.13)	(0.14)	(0.13)
Household income	0.06	0.01	–0.01	0.02
	(0.04)	(0.03)	(0.03)	(0.03)
Parental education	–0.01	0.08*	0.11**	0.10**
	(0.05)	(0.04)	(0.05)	(0.04)
Change in school to parent	0.25***	0.20***	0.31***	0.35***
contact about	(0.07)	(0.06)	(0.06)	(0.05)
volunteering				
Year indicators				
1990	1.39***	–0.42**	0.41**	0.55***
	(0.20)	(0.17)	(0.16)	(0.16)
1991	0.37*	0.08	0.01	0.19
	(0.19)	(0.17)	(0.17)	(0.17)
1993	0.21	–0.18	0.18	0.15
	(0.21)	(0.18)	(0.19)	(0.18)
1994	–0.28	–0.06	–0.16	–0.21
	(0.20)	(0.22)	(0.23)	(.22)
N	387	387	387	387
R^2	—	—	—	0.23
Constant	—	—	—	–0.80 (0.25)
Cut points	–0.77	–0.38	–0.27	—
	1.60	1.39	1.69	—
Wald chi^2(8)	108.32	40.18	59.68	—
Prob > chi^2	0.00	0.00	0.00	—

Source: Data from Witte and Thorn 1995.

Note: Columns 1 through 3 present ordered probit regression results. Column 4 presents ordinary least squares (OLS) regression results. Standard error estimates are in parentheses.The dependent variable in columns 1 through 3 is derived by subtracting the fall report of belonging to the PTA, attending PTA meetings, and active participation in the PTA (covering the previous school year) from the spring report about the current year. The dependent variable in column 4 is a summary of these changes. Positive coefficient estimates are associated with an increased participation, controlling for other predictors.

*$p < 0.1$;   **$p < .05$;   ***$p < .01$, two-tailed.

case, I examine the probabilities that parents who did not belong to the PTA, attend its meetings, or get involved with its activities last year did this year, as a function of whether they were accepted into the voucher program or not. Table 2.4 presents these simulation results. Though there is some overlap in the estimated confidence intervals on these probabilities, it is clear from the results in table 2.4 that the statistically significant coefficient estimates from table 2.3 indicate significant real-world consequences as well. Accepted parents were nearly twice as likely to increase their participation in these areas as a result of their acceptance into the program. It is also likely—since the underlying model included school-to-parent contact about volunteering—that at least some of these gains are brought about by changes in the patterns of parental participation rather than only due to the efforts of the private schools.

By examining the predicted probabilities of participation changes brought about by acceptance into the voucher program as a function of socioeconomic status of participants and nonparticipants, it is possible to see if the processes of social capital building within the choice community are differentially effective, a possibility that has not yet been sufficiently explored in the literature. I focus on two salient characteristics—the family household income and the level of parental education—to see if the participatory benefits are equally shared by those who are more and less well-off. Table 2.5 presents the predicted probabilities of changes in the mean PTA summary measure—which takes on values from –3 to 3—for three groups of voucher applicants: those with mean household incomes,

TABLE 2.4. Probabilities of Participating: Choice Accepted versus Choice Rejected

	Mean (1)	Standard Error (2)	95% Confidence Interval (3)
Probability that parent			
Did not belong to PTA last year but did this year			
Choice accepted	0.27	(0.03)	[0.22–0.33]
Choice rejected	0.18	(0.03)	[0.12–0.25]
Did not attend PTA meetings last year but did this year			
Choice accepted	0.28	(0.03)	[0.23–0.33]
Choice rejected	0.15	(0.03)	[0.10–0.21]
Was not active in PTA last year but was this year			
Choice accepted	0.29	(0.03)	[0.24–0.35]
Choice rejected	0.15	(0.03)	[0.10–0.21]

Source: Data from Witte and Thorn 1995.
Note: Probabilities obtained using Clarify (see King, Tomz, and Wittenberg 2000).

those in the lower quartile of household income, and those at the top quartile.[34] Table 2.6 presents a similar analysis according to the level of parental education.[35]

The social capital–building effects of enrolling in the Milwaukee voucher program do not appear to be related to household income. While choice-accepted gain more than choice-rejected, the patterns between high- and low-income parents do not differ. This is not surprising, since

TABLE 2.5.   Expected Changes in Participation and Household Income: Choice Accepted and Choice Rejected

Expected One-Year Change in Total PTA Participation (may take on values from –3 to 3)	Mean (1)	Standard Error (2)	95% Confidence Interval (3)
Average values of income			
Choice accepted	0.61	(0.06)	[0.47–0.73]
Choice rejected	–0.01	(0.11)	[–0.21–0.19]
Lower quartile of household income			
Choice accepted	0.58	(0.07)	[0.43–0.74]
Choice rejected	–0.04	(0.11)	[–0.26–0.18]
Upper quartile of household income			
Choice accepted	0.64	(0.08)	[0.48–0.77]
Choice rejected	0.02	(0.14)	[–0.21–0.25]

Source: Data from Witte and Thorn 1995.
Note: Probabilities obtained using Clarify (see King, Tomz, and Wittenberg 2000).

TABLE 2.6.   Expected Changes in Participation and Parental Education: Choice Accepted and Choice Rejected

Expected One-Year Change in Total PTA Participation (may take on values from –3 to 3)	Mean (1)	Standard Error (2)	95% Confidence Interval (3)
Average values education			
Choice accepted	0.61	(0.06)	[0.47–0.73]
Choice rejected	–0.01	(0.11)	[–0.21–0.19]
Lower quartile of parental education			
Choice accepted	0.39	(0.12)	[0.14–0.63]
Choice rejected	–0.23	(0.14)	[–0.48–0.04]
Upper quartile of parental education			
Choice accepted	0.64	(0.08)	[0.48–0.77]
Choice rejected	0.16	(0.14)	[–0.10–0.43]

Source: Data from Witte and Thorn 1995.
Note: Probabilities obtained using Clarify (see King, Tomz, and Wittenberg 2000).

having an income less than or equal to 1.75 times the level of poverty is a prerequisite to acceptance into the program. An annual household income of $15,000 qualifies a household for the upper income quartile in these simulations. Even within this population, however, benefits of acceptance into the program are closely related to the educational attainment of the participant. While even choice-rejected parents at the upper end of the education distribution are likely to show gains in participation, choice-accepted parents in the lower quartile of educational attainment are only expected to show about two-thirds of the gains as parents at the mean or top quartile of educational attainment. Choice-rejected parents with less education are expected to show declines in participation over the course of the year. These results complicate the possibility that private choice programs will produce uniform benefits in the process of social capital formation. Concerns about the connection between socioeconomic status and participatory benefits are most relevant when one considers the possibility that these programs may one day be expanded considerably to include more middle-income families.

Resource Inequalities, Participation, and Choice

We know that wealthier and more highly educated individuals are more likely to engage in the broad range of activities that define political participation.[36] These disparities in participation result in a biased and incomplete representation in American democracy. The disparities are especially problematic when one places them in the context of creating healthy democratic communities, a process that is inherently dynamic and self-reinforcing.[37] That these processes are dynamic at the individual level suggests that their aggregation, in the form of community building, might be similarly dynamic, a phenomenon described by scholars as a vicious-virtuous cycle, in which the destruction of social capital, if left unchecked, can feed on itself.[38]

What has not been discussed in this focus on differences in the absolute value of voice in rich and poor communities is the possibility of a more complicated relationship between the benefits and volume of voice. Poor communities—which we know have less absolute participation to begin with—might stand the most to lose if the activist voices that they do have leave. The processes of social capital formation, sustenance, and destruction may play out differently in resource-rich and resource-poor communities. Private sector exit in education, I argue, changes the dynamics of civic engagement and social capital formation, and these effects are more destructive for poorer communities. This is an important way in which the self-interested behavior of parents looking for the best possible education for their children can damage the larger democratic community.

This chapter's final analysis consists of a simulation aimed at exploring the possible effects of a large expansion of both private and public school choice policies and connecting these potential effects to resource inequalities. These data come from the 1996 National Household Education Survey, a large-sample telephone survey of parents and students on questions of civic development and political participation. As part of the larger survey, parents of students in sixth through twelfth grade were asked questions about their own civic involvement as well as about the type of schooling one selected child was receiving.[39] More than 75 percent of parents in the survey reported sending their children to assigned public schools, with the rest of parents split between private schools and public choice schools.

It is important to note that these surveys do not capture the effects of the two most discussed policies that are currently in use to facilitate exit to the private sector (voucher programs) or within the public sector (charter schools). The year in which these data were collected, 1996, was, in many ways, part of the Paleolithic, or at least the Neolithic, era of school choice. Though they include parents who were sending their children to magnet and public school choice options, the surveys do not ask parents if they are participating in a voucher program or sending their child to a charter school. I cannot, therefore, use these data to evaluate the effects of these two specific choice options. What I can do, however, is to use the data to look for differences between those parents who may or may not be more likely to enroll their children in public or private schools. These simulation results, therefore, can be used to highlight potentially different results from exit to the public and private sectors and to enrich the discussion of how sector, parental education, and income within a given sector will matter to any potential expansion of school choice policies in the United States.

In addition to asking about student placement, the survey included an extensive list of questions about parents' involvement with their children's schools in the larger political community, along with a vector of demographic characteristics. The first step in my analysis is to construct two models of school choice, in which the act of opting out of one's assigned public school, whether through enrolling one's child in a public choice program or sending the child to a private school, is treated as a function of a parent's school and political participation and his or her individual sociodemographic characteristics.[40]

I am primarily interested in using the coefficient estimates to make predictions for the simulation. However, there are some clear patterns in the data.[41] Though parents who send their children to private schools tend to have higher incomes, parents who choose public school choice are actually likely to have lower incomes than a comparable group of parents who send their children to traditional public schools. This makes sense, as most public choice programs are in inner cities, and many wealthier parents have paid a premium to purchase access to high-quality suburban public schools. More educated parents, however, are more likely to leave the traditional public schools, a finding consistent with both the literature on school choice and the findings regarding the Milwaukee parental choice program. This is going to be important, as more educated parents, regardless of income levels, are more likely to be activist parents.

There is also strong evidence that parents who have exited are different in their involvement with their schools and political communities. Those parents who have left for either a public choice or private school option are more involved in their school communities. All of these relationships are statistically significant. As these are static data, it is not possible to separate out the processes of skimming and social capital formation as I did with the Milwaukee choice program data. I cannot say if parents who choose not to enroll their child in an assigned public school were more efficacious and participatory when they made the decision or because of it. Given the results from the Milwaukee data, however, it is likely that it is some of both.

The second step in the analysis is to use fitted values from the regression to predict a probability of leaving the public schools for each parent who remains in the assigned public schools. Each public school parent, in other words, is ranked according to the likelihood that they will enroll their child in either a public choice or a private school. Of course these parents have not exited; they all report sending their children to assigned public schools. The point is to rank them on the likelihood that they might leave, based on similarities to those parents who have already left.

By sequentially deleting the public school parents who are most likely to leave and then examining the characteristics of those parents remaining in the sample, it is possible to simulate the expected changes in political participation of public school parents as more and more parents leave for public and private choice options, and to see if these likely changes will depend on the socioeconomic status of the school community. This allows me to investigate the potential effects of the departure of the activist parents on the use of voice as a means of institutional control in the remaining public schools, knowing that, in relative terms, these effects may only

understate the potential challenges to public schools presented by private choice programs. The results of these simulations are only predicted probabilities, using what we know about the characteristics of parents who do exit to make predictions about what will happen if many more leave. They are illustrative but cannot, of course, be used to accept or reject any hypotheses. As discussed, however, where those parents go is critical to the institutional consequences of choice, as parents' participatory resources are either retained within the public system or removed from it.

Figure 2.1 presents the simulated effects of school choice on the distribution of parental involvement within the public schools. The two components of the school participation variable from the regression stage of the simulation are used: whether the parent has volunteered at school or on a committee and whether the parent has attended a teacher conference during the school year. As one moves right along the horizontal axis, higher percentages of parents in the public school sample are deleted, based on their similarities with parents who have already have done so. The choice of 20 percent exit is somewhat arbitrary, and perhaps controversial. Few choice programs in the United States even approach enrolling 20 percent of the kindergarten through grade twelve students in the United States. However, advocates for both charters and vouchers encourage their expansion, and I will be careful to comment on the simulated consequences that arise from lower levels of exit.

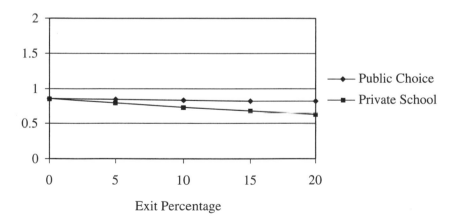

FIG. 2.1. The expansion of choice and parental involvement in the public schools. The x-axis depicts the percentage of public school parents deleted from the sample, based on their predicted probability of leaving. The y-axis depicts school participation score, derived by giving a parent one point for having attended a teacher conference or having volunteered at school within the past year. (Data from 1996 National Household Education Survey.)

The expansion of school choice is likely to present a loss of parental involvement for the assigned public schools, but this loss will depend on what kind of a school the parent and his or her student exits to. The probability of a parent volunteering time and energy at his or her child's school declines by only 3.5 percent in the case of exit within the public sector, but by nearly 26 percent if parents who are more likely to leave for the private schools have done so. Even given the more modest possibility that no more than 5 percent of parents leave, the public schools will experience a decline of 7 percent in parental involvement in the schools in the case of exit to the private sector, and just over 1 percent in the case of public school exit. Not only may the expansion of private options drain more activist parents from individual public schools, but these resources are lost to the public school system as well. Given the importance of even a small number of active parents within and surrounding the schools, these potential losses might be even more significant than the simulations suggest.

These simulations also suggest declines in political participation beyond the school walls and in the larger community (fig. 2.2). For the political participation variable, parents were given one point for having, within the past year, written or telephoned an editor or public official about an issue, attended a public meeting, participated in a community

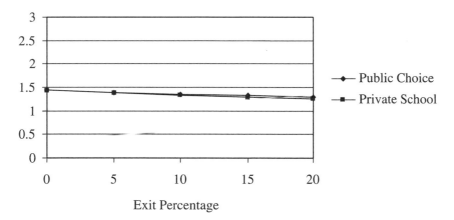

Exit Percentage

FIG. 2.2. The expansion of choice and parental political participation. The x-axis depicts the percentage of public school parents deleted from the sample, based on their predicted probability of leaving. The y-axis depicts the political participation score, derived by giving a parent one point for having, within the past year, written or telephoned an editor or public official about an issue, attended a public meeting, participated in a community service activity, worked for pay or as a volunteer for a candidate or political party, or participated in a protest or boycott. (Data from 1996 National Household Education Survey.)

service activity, worked for pay or as a volunteer for a candidate or political party, or participated in a protest or boycott. The relative declines in political participation are similar, suggesting that private and public exit will have similar school-level effects on the expression of voice in the larger political community. At a simulated exit of 20 percent, each option reduces the political scores of parents by roughly 5 percent. At 5 percent exit, the decline is about 3.5 percent.

The parents who are leaving may be the very people to whom schools turn when they need votes in a budget election or are trying to marshal support for curricular innovation. Not only would the political resources of the departed parents no longer be available to the public schools, they might be used against the public schools over issues in which choice programs were competing with traditional public schools, such as the relative level of regulation between the two. The results of these two simulations suggest that there may be important institutional implications from private choice programs, particularly if they are expanded significantly. These simulations cannot determine where the parents who have left for the private schools will apply their political skills. It is possible that they will continue to work toward improving the public schools that they have left behind by participating in school elections and attending school board meetings, but they may not do so with the same level of energy, given the incentives to focus on their children's new private schools.

Having traced out the expected effects of expanding public and private school choice programs on parental activism in a way that treats all public school communities equally, I conclude by exploring the potential that the consequences of parental exit will be different for resource-rich and resource-poor communities. The analysis relies on the same regressions as before. However, in the second stage, I split the original sample of public school parents into quartiles based on their reported household income and level of parental education. I then conduct the simulations as before, tracing out expected patterns of participation for the lowest and highest quartiles of the public school parent sample for household income and parental education respectively. One way to think about these simulations is that I have artificially constructed resource-rich and resource-poor school communities so that I may examine the consequences of public and private exit on the expression of voice within them.

Figure 2.3 presents the predicted mean school participation scores for the highest and lowest quartiles of the public school parent sample, based on household income. Recall that the school participation variable is coded from zero to two, with one point being given for attending a meeting at school and one point for volunteering at the child's school within the

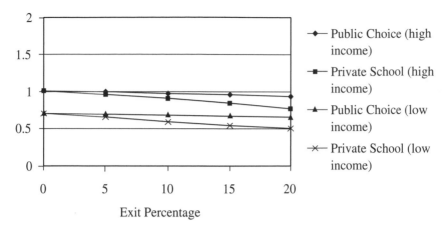

FIG. 2.3. Choice skimming and school participation, by household income. The x-axis depicts the percentage of public school parents deleted from the sample, based on their predicted probability of leaving. The y-axis depicts school participation score, derived by giving a parent one point for having attended a teacher conference or having volunteered at school within the past year. (Data from 1996 National Household Education Survey.)

past year. As before, the exit percentage is increasing on the horizontal axis, with increasingly large percentages of parents deleted as one moves to the right side of the figure.

The first thing to note is that lower-income parents begin with lower levels of school participation than higher-income parents, which is what one would expect. These differences, however, are not trivial. Lower-income parents, before selecting out the most likely to exit, have school participation scores 30 percent lower than their higher-income counterparts. In addition, the relative declines in school participation from the simulated private school exit are much higher than for public school exit. The expansion of public school choice options does not appear to result in declines in school participation, and there do not appear to be significant differences in declines between higher- and lower-income parents from expanding exit within the public sector.

The predictions for expanding exit to the private schools, however, are quite different. It is somewhat difficult to see in the graph; however, the percentage declines in school participation arising from private school exit are higher for the lower-income quartile than for the higher-income quartile. At 20 percent exit to private schools, the average school participation score declines by 30 percent in the lower-income quartile. The similar declines from private school exit in the upper-income quartile, however, are 24 percent.

I find similar patterns of decline in the effects of exit on school participation when comparing parents based on their educational attainment (fig. 2.4). The differences between higher and lower levels of education, between public and private exit, and in the interaction of education and sector repeat the troubling patterns observed in the high- and low-income parents. Parents in the bottom quartile of parental education start out with school participation scores 28 percent lower than their more educated counterparts. The expansion of public choice, though leading to a 5 percent decline in school participation, does not appear to have more serious effects on parent communities with lower levels of education.

The expansion of private choice options, however, results in a decline of school participation of 23 percent for the more educated subset of parents and a nearly 32 percent decline in school participation for the less educated school community. Though these are only simulations, they suggest that poorer communities and those with lower levels of education—which begin with lower levels of school participation—may suffer more from an expansion of private choice policies than higher-income and more educated communities do. If the costs to poorer communities of an equal loss of activist voices is disproportionately large—if they need their activists more than the resource-rich districts do—then these consequences will only be magnified.

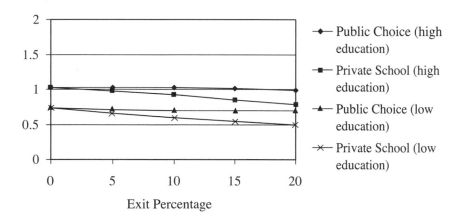

FIG. 2.4. Choice skimming and school participation, by parental education. The x-axis depicts the percentage of public school parents deleted from the sample, based on their predicted probability of leaving. The y-axis depicts school participation score, derived by giving a parent one point for having attended a teacher conference or having volunteered at school within the past year. (Data from 1996 National Household Education Survey.)

The final piece of the puzzle is to compare the effects of exit within and beyond the public school system on the larger political participation of parents, according to their household incomes (fig. 2.5) and level of education (fig. 2.6). The differences in initial participation for the resource-rich and resource-poor communities repeat the differences that I observed in school participation. Lower-income and less-educated public school parents begin the analysis with political participation scores that are less than half those of their wealthier and more-educated counterparts.

Unlike the case of school participation, there are not significant differences between the declines according to whether the parent exits to the private sector or within the public sector. In fact, the declines in political participation are actually slightly worse for the low-income public choice programs (22 percent) than for the private school exit (18 percent). In the case of skimming and lower levels of parental education, however, private school exit is associated with a slightly higher level of skimming (a 14 percent decline in political participation) than for the exit to public schools (an 11 percent decline), patterns more consistent with the school participation analyses. Recall, however, that the Milwaukee program is targeted at low-income parents.

Based on these simulation results, it is likely that a large expansion of school choice policies—at least those that facilitate exit from the public

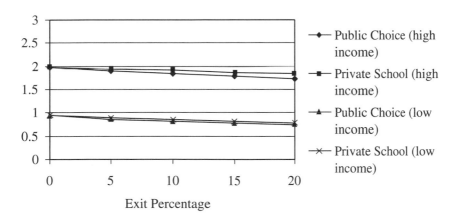

FIG. 2.5. Choice skimming and political participation, by household income. The x-axis depicts the percentage of public school parents deleted from the sample, based on their predicted probability of leaving. The y-axis depicts the political participation score, derived by giving a parent one point for having, within the past year, written or telephoned an editor or public official about an issue, attended a public meeting, participated in a community service activity, worked for pay or as a volunteer for a candidate or political party, or participated in a protest or boycott. (Data from 1996 National Household Education Survey.)

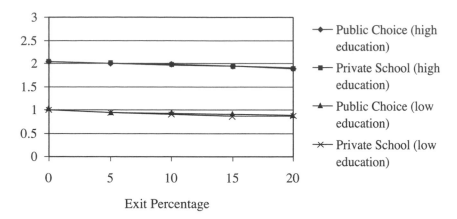

FIG. 2.6.   Choice skimming and political participation, by parental education. The x-axis depicts the percentage of public school parents deleted from the sample, based on their predicted probability of leaving. The y-axis depicts the political participation score, derived by giving a parent one point for having, within the past year, written or telephoned an editor or public official about an issue, attended a public meeting, participated in a community service activity, worked for pay or as a volunteer for a candidate or political party, or participated in a protest or boycott. (Data from 1996 National Household Education Survey.)

system—is going to produce significant drains on individual schools and less substantial, though perhaps nontrivial, drains on the political participation of the public school parent communities. These effects are going to be much more significant in those communities with less active parent communities, challenging the hopeful prospect for bureaucratic reinvigoration in those schools that need it the most.

Conclusions

The evidence from the Milwaukee school choice program is consistent with both skimming and social capital–building arguments. Self-selection of activist parents and social capital building on the part of choosers are taking place simultaneously. An active subset of parents is more likely to exit when offered the choice, even in a targeted choice program, and the political participation of these choosers changes in response to their participation. The results of the simulations in the second part of the chapter indicate that processes of social capital formation and destruction will depend both on the structure of the choice program and on the preexisting resources of these communities. Lower-income and less-educated communities are going to see significantly larger drains on the involvement of parent communities, particularly for policies that facilitate exit to the private sector. It appears that those who warn against skimming and those who argue for social capital formation are both partly correct. However, neither perspective has considered the possibility that both skimming and social capital formation are occurring simultaneously or the possibility that these processes will have different effects on different communities of parents.

In the case of policies that facilitate exit from the public sector, the synergy of these processes might be more dangerous to the public schools than the presence of skimming by itself. From the point of view of the relative ability of public school parents to control and support their public schools compared to those parents within the choice options, either the skimming effect or the social capital–building process would produce a relatively disadvantaged public school parent group. If, however, one considers the ability of parents to control and advocate for their public schools relative to the ability of parents in private choice options to do the same, then either the presence of self-selection or increased political participation on the part of active choosers will make the public schools relatively worse off, either by draining the most active parents or by advantaging the choice options as their parents become relatively more active.

The possibility that both processes might be at work would only magnify these relative deficiencies, as private choice options skim the most active parents and encourage them to become even more active in the process, further disadvantaging the public schools competing in the policy space. On any political battle that is going to pit the public schools against the voucher-accepting private schools (such as the relative level of regulation of the two), the public schools are going to be operating without their most effective parents, and those parents who have now moved to the private schools are going to be even more effective in the exercise of their political skills. If the market model of bureaucratic responsiveness is too narrow in that it ignores the community-building aspects of the public school principalship, it is also too simplistic as it treats all customers as equals. Some customers may have more financial resources than others, but, after all, one person's money is not of higher quality than another's. This is not true in the world of politics. Some people are more effective in their participation, regardless of how much participating they are doing.

The analyses in this chapter provide evidence to support the claim that the systemic effects of market forces and parental participation will be meaningfully different depending on whether parents have choices within or beyond the public sector. Much research remains to be done. Though I examined the comparative consequences on parental behaviors for systems of public and private school choice, I have not yet examined the institutional consequences of these changes in behaviors and levels of social capital. I will not be providing any evidence for or against the possibility that public schools, under pressure from voucher programs, might attempt to respond to this competition by reaching out to their customers. I believe that they will, and this prediction is entirely consistent with beneficial bureaucratic consequences of exit. There is nothing in the literature that shows that they have done so, though voucher programs are new, and no researchers have systematically studied this potential process. The lack of evidence for beneficial bureaucratic consequences arising from private voucher programs does not mean that they do not exist.

I argue, however, that there is a much bigger distinction between public and private choice than the question of which one scares the public school bureaucrats more. It is all about resources. Under voucher programs, public schools have fewer, and so—if one accepts my foundational assumption that parents constitute an important part of public school resources—voucher programs threaten the public schools' parental resources. Any social capital–building benefits that arise from private voucher programs will not accrue to the public school communities and may very well be used against them on issues that pit the public and the private space against each other.

At this point, I am going to leave the private schools behind. My focus for the rest of the book will be on charter schools. They are more complicated, interesting, and promising in terms of the potential for marketlike reforms to result in beneficial bureaucratic and democratic effects. I have no reason to think that the same processes of skimming and social capital building that I observe in the case of the Milwaukee voucher program will not be displayed in the case of charter schools. In fact, I will argue that they do, and will present, in some detail, evidence that this is the case. The larger point is which sector, public or private, is going to benefit from these potentially beneficial transformations.

3 | Over the Principal's Shoulder

> Political scientists ought to learn about politicians by talking
> to them, watching them and following them around. Some
> research can be done by bringing politicians—aspiring, active,
> or retired—to the academic work place. But most of it must
> be done in the setting in which politicians operate, in their
> natural habitats. The aim is to see the world as they see it, to
> adopt their vantage point on politics. For it is precisely this
> view, from over the politician's shoulder, that is now missing
> from political science research.
>
> —*Richard F. Fenno Jr.,* Watching Politicians[1]

"WE TOOK EIGHTY KIDS on an orchestra trip to Europe," one of the New
Jersey public school principals in my study tells me. "The kids were mar-
velous."

His is a high school in a wealthy suburban district, with a statewide reputation for academic excellence. His school is financed primarily by local
property taxes on single-family homes. His district has one charter school
already established in it, although the charter does not currently enroll
high school students. He has tenure, with thirteen years of experience, and
expresses confidence about his relations with his parent community.

> I gave them [the students] feedback each night. Flexibility and free-
> dom were related to responsibility. [Late in the trip] they asked me,
> "Can we go to a disco?" There were two discos, one was at our hotel
> . . . closer, safer, in town.
>
> We were shuttling kids in. Then the manager announced that the
> strip show would be starting in five minutes. I asked the manager to
> delay the show for a few minutes, and offered to pay for the incon-
> venience.

The students were gone before the stage show began. The principal tells
me that he was never concerned about how this was going to play out back
in New Jersey.[2]

49

It was fine. When we got back I heard from one of the kids, "[Our principal] is the only person ever to pay someone not to strip." The kids wrote it up in the school paper. For weeks I was meeting people in the supermarket and getting kidded about it. Those kinds of stories, if they're managed well, go into the basic lore of the school.

The lesson conveyed, in his view, not a potential scandal, but the professionalism, awareness, and flexibility of a public administrator entrusted with a great deal of responsibility. These stories produce, for this principal, a currency that he feels he can use to buy his larger vision for the school, a currency most valuable among a small group of wealthy and involved parents. This kind of story, he tells me, plays well to these customers.

The parents who will be the most vocal are the parents who are going to get served. The cost of helping everybody else is the challenge of taking on the top income parents. I invest in them. I educate them. I make sure all of that is taken care of. If you don't, you can't get stuff done.

For this principal, "stuff" means taking care to see that the needs of the minority of poor kids in his district are also being adequately met. He feels that this is part of what defines him as a professional. The trust he builds with a wealthy and involved subset of the parents in the neighborhood facilitates his ability to help the entire community.

I have a summer school program that I raise money for independently. . . . I've been the principal in communities where the parents are not involved. The good side is the autonomy. You have more freedom to implement your vision, provided you have the resources. The bad side is the same. You never have the resources. The importance of reputation can't be underestimated. People will give you the benefit of the doubt. That's what it buys you.

This principal consciously connects his ability to take care of all of his students to the stories that emerge from his school and his actions, the information he sends to his parent community about his abilities and the quality of the services he provides. Some of these stories are targeted at the more highly informed and wealthy parents, a group that he views as vital resources to implementing his vision for the school. That principals work to build a trust with the wealthy and involved parents, which they can then barter for things they really care about, is strikingly similar to what Richard F. Fenno Jr. (1978) observed about representatives in their districts. Members work their districts to gain trust to allow freedom of movement in the vote. That Fenno and I find similar strategies among the political actors that we observe speaks to one of the strengths of qualitative analysis: it allows a deeper understanding of political strategies as the actors perceive them.

For this public school principal, his active customers may never be able to perfectly and objectively measure the true quality of his principalship, even if he ever could. And there exists a considerable degree of uncertainty surrounding the transmission and reception of his stories and the information he hopes to convey. Stories are managed, not controlled. Any parent who can help a principal get the word out or take the pulse of the community has something very useful to offer.

Another principal framed his communication with his parent community in a similar way, for him in terms of the messages he sends.

Do the messages get through? Yes. How accurate are they? That's another question. A few years ago I brought in a P.R. consultant to do an assessment of our school. He said I wasn't visible enough. I told him I go to every football game. I walk the building three periods a day. He said that's not what it's about. It's about perception.

I've been in this district for thirty-one years. I like to believe I have a good rapport with the community, a reputation for being a disciplinarian. That reputation helps me run a tight ship.

For another school principal, in one of the poorest districts in the state, the parental networks are much less specific, much more uncertain. She attributes this lack of specificity to the fact that this is her first year as the principal of this new school, though she has many years of experience as principal of another, larger school in this district. This job is a chance to make an impact, she tells me, but there is much work to be done. She is having trouble getting parent involvement and is still experiencing low attendance at the Parent Action Committee meetings she schedules.

Performance, for her, is the key to increasing parental activism: "If all my kindergartners could read, the word would get out. The parents would go to the board or the superintendent." After eight months, however, she tells me that her parent network remains a vague and unspecific thing. "Parents are way in the background here. They won't tell you what they think. They might tell the security guard."

How do parents matter in education? We know that parental involvement is critical to a child's success in school,[3] but less attention has been paid to the many ways that parents get involved other than helping their children with their homework.

For this small group of public school principals in New Jersey, considerations of what parental activism means and how it is expressed suggest some important points that researchers of the effects of school choice on the public schools should consider more carefully. Parents can matter, but parental involvement is much more complicated than simply showing up at a PTA meeting. The way principals attend to and organize their parents can matter as well. The resources that parents can bring to a school principal in his or her efforts toward attaining a vision of the good school may be important as well. Activism, however, is expressed heterogeneously, both within a school's parent community and between the parent communities of different schools and districts. Some parents matter more than others, and it is not at all clear that this activism is independent of race, class, or educational attainment within or across public school communities. My goal in this chapter is to explore these complexities in more detail.

Soaking and Poking in New Jersey

The title of this chapter, "Over the Principal's Shoulder," refers both to the object of my study—the ways in which principals' behaviors are constrained or enhanced by the parent community watching over and guiding them—and to one of the research methods employed—that of observational study of politicians in the workplace. This kind of contextual study is well suited to learning how perceptions of constraint might influence the behaviors and calculations of public bureaucrats. During the 1999–2000 school year, I conducted observational studies of six public school principals in New Jersey, each confronting public school choice in his or her district, whether through the presence of one or more charter schools in the district or through involvement in the state's small interdistrict public choice program.

The object was to observe the principals in their most public contexts, in the school board, PTA, district, and governance meetings, along with an assortment of dinners, ceremonies, plays, concerts, and events, and to meet with the principals before and after to understand better how they view their constituency, how they anticipate these interactions, and how they interpret them afterward. For Richard F. Fenno Jr., this kind of observational study of politicians is crucial to understanding the effects of context on behavior: "In order to observe politicians, you must operate in an unfamiliar context. And that basic condition drives you, inevitably, to a sharpened appreciation of *context* as a variable in your analysis."[4]

"Politicians at work" is the phrase Nelson Polsby attached to the objects of Fenno's studies, and the phrase is appropriate here as well.[5] If public school principals in their schools are politicians at work, then school principals confronting choice policies are politicians in a transforming workplace. Finding out how politicians get their work done, for Polsby, entails finding out how the incentive structures under which they operate determines their choices and channels their ambitions. To understand the effects of school choice on bureaucratic responsiveness requires the same kind of contextual understanding and the same kind of focus on incentive structures to which Fenno and Polsby refer.

We know that public school principals are being asked to respond to new incentives with the introduction of school choice reforms. For many of these individuals, responding to these changes involves new ways of doing things that might not have been covered in their professional training. The ground-level responses of public school principals to the introduction of market forces are also relatively new to scholars of public administration. In order to better understand these bureaucratic responses, I went out to watch over the shoulders of a diverse group of public school principals in a variety of settings and contexts in order to help frame questions for the empirical studies that follow.

I contacted by telephone and mail thirty-two public school principals in New Jersey who were facing choice in their district, either through the presence of a charter school or through participation in the state's interdistrict public choice program. In choosing the thirty-two, I concentrated on ensuring a diverse group representing core urban areas, suburban middle-class areas, and wealthier communities. Six agreed to let me follow them around over an extended period of time to observe and dissect some very public moments.[6]

I studied two schools at each level: elementary, middle, and high. Of these six schools, three were in the inner city, two were working-class and middle-class small town and suburban settings, and one was in a wealthy suburb. According to New Jersey's standardized ten-point ranking of the wealth of the state's more than six hundred school districts, two of my schools were in the poorest level, one in the richest, and the others in-between. One district received more than 80 percent of its funding from the state; another, less than 10 percent. The smallest school, an elementary school, enrolled just over two hundred students; the largest, a high school, more than a thousand. Student achievement and test score results were equally diverse. I made fifty visits to these six schools, spending more than a hundred hours at the schools, either meeting with the principal, accompanying him or her to a meeting or event, or discussing it before and or afterward. In one case, I was only able to spend a few short but important hours with the principal; in three cases, more than twenty-four.

I begin with my analysis of one of the most promising reforms that introduces marketlike competition within the system of public schools: the charter school. Of course it is not possible to generalize from these six cases, and one cannot compare principals encountering choice with those not encountering choice, as the small number would not allow much leverage on this question and would not allow any leverage on the comparative behavior of principals encountering private choice, as New Jersey does not have a private voucher program. For Richard F. Fenno Jr., the goal of his observational studies was to "open up" his subject of how legislators think about their world "for scholarly inquiry."[7] My claims are much more modest, partly because there is already a rich observational literature within educational policy studies,[8] and partly because I cannot hope to settle empirical debates based only on observing a small group of principals in one state experiencing choice within the public sector only. I am almost certain that these individuals are anything but a representative sample of New Jersey public school principals. Although they are a diverse group in terms of gender, race, and ethnicity, these individuals are, in all likelihood, a highly confident and competent subset of the thousands of public school principals in New Jersey.

What I can do with these observational studies, however, is to set up and guide the empirical analyses that follow, to begin to explore how school principals think about and interact with their citizens and customers in the real world, using their constituents as resources in achieving their goals for their schools and students. The interview and observational data taught me a great deal about principals' perceptions of the system of relationships in which they are embedded, as distinct from the ways theorists might think principals view their worlds. It allowed me to better trace the pathways through which activism, autonomy, and constraint are expressed for public school principals and their parent communities, to reflect on the ways choice might interact with or alter these pathways and processes, and to think more thoroughly about the implications of market reforms for the bureaucratic autonomy of principals and their responsiveness to their shifting parent communities.

New Jersey's Experiment with Choice

The idea that market reforms might improve New Jersey's public schools was brought to the public agenda during the fall of 1992, when Democratic governor Jim Florio supported a bipartisan bill that would introduce a new kind of public school to New Jersey: the charter school. Florio pointed to charter school legislation such as that which had already passed in Minnesota and California, as giving hope to the state's most troubled public schools.

The main idea of a charter school is that its leaders are primarily accountable to the charter, the founding document, rather than to the local school board or state education bureaucracy. That freedom varies by state, but it is never absolute; many rules covering health, safety, and nondiscrimination apply equally to the charters and public schools. Some states place restrictions on who can start charter schools; however, it is possible in some states for profit-seeking corporations to participate in or manage charter schools even if they are not allowed to start them alone. Charter schools are publicly funded. Typically, they receive their money from the student's home district.

Florio's opponent in the 1993 gubernatorial race, Christine Todd Whitman, suggested a more radical plan, one that had been floated by Bret Schundler, a Harvard-educated investment adviser, former Democrat, and the first Republican mayor of Jersey City since 1917. The plan included the introduction of public school choice in the state and a pilot program giving every parent in Jersey City a voucher to attend any school, public or private, within the city.

Following her election, Governor Whitman proposed a voucher plan to the state assembly and senate. The New Jersey Education Association, which had been fighting Schundler's proposal in the courts, soon raised ten million dollars to lobby against Whitman's proposals. In response, the governor agreed to delay any voucher legislation for one year and scaled back the proposed Jersey City voucher program to serve only first and ninth graders in the city. She also added a charter schools proposal to her reform package. Charter schools were popular in the state and were not as fiercely opposed by the unions, provided that the number of charter schools approved would be limited. By late 1995 the voucher plan had been shelved, and the emphasis had been moved entirely to charter schools. A bipartisan bill, the Charter School Program Act, passed the state legislature late in 1995 and was signed into law by Governor Whitman in 1996.

The initial legislation capped the number of charter schools in the state at one hundred and thirty-five. Each charter school must have its charter renewed every four years. There are restrictions placed on private ownership or management, and only state-certified teachers can teach in charter schools. The schools are not allowed to exclude by ability or handicap, or include on the basis of academics or athletics, a big concern for many top public football programs in the state. They must assign spots on the basis of a lottery if there are more applicants than spaces.

In 1998 a much restricted public school choice plan passed the assembly and senate, designed to allow students to attend public schools in other districts. Only one district per county was allowed to participate, and students would have to be admitted on a lottery basis. Six of the state's public schools were selected for the pilot choice program. Receiving districts only got state aid in the amount available from their own district, removing financial incentives for some wealthy schools to take poorer students. There was little excitement for or against the public choice plan, as neither side expected it to have much of an impact. The biggest support came from overcrowded districts, which might prefer to send students out rather than build new schools, and those with dwindling enrollment, which were happy to have more students and funds.

Charter schools are designed to introduce more competition into the public system, but it would be incorrect to assume that this competition will only take market forms, in that the public schools will primarily strive to make better products. The public school system may also fight back politically, and the degree to which school choice makes public school players more politically savvy is beginning to be explored in the literature.[9] Political opposition by New Jersey school boards to charter proposals in their districts was quick and intense. The charter school legislation allowed school board opposition to be considered by the commissioner in granting or rejecting charters but did not bind the commissioner to follow the local school board's advice. In 1997, five school boards successfully appealed two of the original charter decisions. In 1998, thirteen of the first twenty-three schools were challenged by local districts, based on a potential loss of revenue and interference in maintaining racial and ethnic diversity within the school system. Several districts sought to block the transfer of funds to the charters. When the state board of education rejected the claims against all thirteen of these charter schools, the local districts went to court.

While most of New Jersey's charter schools opened in urban areas with the goal of serving poor and minority students, there remained a great deal of diversity in funding, emphasis, scope, and structure in the charter programs. In general it did not appear that charters were serving only elite children. Rather, a 1998 Columbia Teachers College study found that 72 percent of New Jersey's charter school students were minorities, and more than half were eligible for free and reduced lunch, much higher than the state public school average.[10] Most charters were opened in inner cities and struggled with facilities and money.

In June 2000, the New Jersey State Supreme Court upheld the constitutionality of the state's charter school legislation, rejecting claims by school districts that charters pose an undue financial hardship on school districts or undercut desegregation efforts. There have been problems at some of the charter schools. Two charter schools have been ordered closed, due to problems in financial management and under accusations of disorganization and violation of state regulations.[11] Four others were placed on probation for similar problems. However, the court's decision ensured that New Jersey's experiment with bringing market forces to the delivery of educational services, itself critically shaped and altered by the political process, would continue.

Autonomy and Constraint

I am in the district superintendent's office of one of my schools, along with the superintendent, two parents, several teachers—one of whom is a union representative—and the principal of one of the district's schools. This principal's elementary school gets most of its money from the state. It has lost eighty students to the local charter school this year, about one per class. Not a critical blow he tells me, but hardly trivial either. The principal has twenty-three years of experience, eleven as a public school teacher, and he has told me several times how stressful his job is. He is not sure he would do it again if given the choice, and more than once he raised the point of some of his colleagues who had suffered heart attacks.

The district superintendent begins the meeting, "Next year we are going to be a pilot district for a new professional development monitoring program."

There are groans.

The pilot project revolves around changing the structure and meaning of the Professional Improvement Program (PIP), a document that outlines the courses, in-services, and other professional development opportunities that each teacher has taken or is planning on taking. The purpose of this meeting is to discuss the new professional development standards handed down by the New Jersey state department of education and this district's role as an early adopter of these changes. This is the first year, the "developmental year," of a statewide process whose aim is to increase regulation and standardization of the continuing education programs and courses in which teachers enroll to maintain certification and move up on the pay scale.

There are three ways for a public school teacher to raise his or her pay when under contract.[12] A teacher can keep teaching and receive the regular step increases in pay that usually come with each increase in seniority. Though there have been trial programs using merit pay, most public school teachers' salaries depend primarily on seniority. Whenever pay is raised for new teachers, everyone else automatically gets more money. A teacher can also move to another district that pays more, although this is usually only an option in one's first few years as a teacher. Districts tend not to hire experienced teachers from other districts, as they usually cost too much.

Teachers may also choose to take courses, attend in-service training sessions and conferences, or obtain an advanced degree. Many districts' salary schedules are laid out as matrices, with one axis specifying years of experience in the district and the other, professional development credits and advanced degrees. Teachers with Ph.D.'s and who have reached maximum seniority in the district are paid the most, rookies with B.A.'s, the least. Most districts also require some number of credits within a fixed time, just to stay employed. The principal feels that the state department's intent in this case is to standardize the process of continuing education, of what counts and what doesn't count on the matrix.

The teachers in the meeting with the district superintendent are worried. They wonder if the in-service training sessions that they have taken this year will count toward their Professional Improvement Programs if they're not on the state's official list, or if they will have to take more courses this summer.

One of the parents is worried, too. She is in charge of some of the development offerings of the local parent-teacher association, half-day events that have, until now, counted toward in-service credit. "If they don't count," she says, looking at the principal, "forget about it. We'll never get our teachers to attend."

The principal explains how the rules constrict his options for counting certain half-day in-services under the new framework. Explaining the rules is a role every one of the public school principals whom I observed assumed at one point or another, and it seemed much more common in the presence of constraint, when requests were denied, ideas rejected. "I got written up because the cheerleaders had a bake sale," one principal in another school said to some of his teachers, parents, and students who wanted to have a fund-raiser. "You can't offer food during lunch hours. If you've got vending machines, you've got to turn them off."

The school principals whom I observed almost always knew more rules better than anyone else in the various meetings I attended, even their administrative superiors. The school principal must deal with a greater diversity of rules than most other actors. Everybody else—parent, teacher, administrator, or board member—may have one or more areas of expertise. But the principal operates at the center of most of these rules systems and so is necessarily a better rules generalist than anyone else.

There is some confusion in the room. It is not clear where the ultimate authority to approve or reject a professional development opportunity lies.

The superintendent turns to the principal.

"Superintendents are hearing [from the state] 'be specific about what programs to put in the PIP.' Teachers are hearing from the union, 'Don't be specific.' You are the one who's going to have to deal with this."

"What does this mean?" asks one of the teachers. "Who decides what counts?"

"It's the decision of the principal," the superintendent replies.

There is silence.

Later, alone in his office, the principal explains to me how concerned he is about the department's latest regulatory effort and the restrictions it will place on his ability to get his teachers to improve in certain areas.

> Before, the teachers didn't have to agree on their PIP. They just had to read it. If there was a problem or a deficiency, I could say to a teacher, in their PIP, "You ought to want to do this." Now, they have to agree to it. If I want to say something to a teacher now, I have to put it in their [official] file. That's a much bigger deal.
>
> The state boards of education have taken over. The people in Trenton have no inkling of what goes on in the classroom. This is the one profession where you get hired on to improve things, but you're saddled with the people you've got. Being principal is like being president; you can no more tell the teachers what to do than the president can tell the senate. And the teachers will outlast you.

There was probably more spoken in that silence than I was aware of. I know now that the principal was not at all happy with his new authority. I suspect that the teachers were sizing up how much leeway they were going to get with the principal, and they weren't very optimistic.

But this awkward little silence illustrates and captures an important part of what common agency means for public school principals. Embeddedness is an essential source of their power as well as a constraint on the exercise of that power. The state department of education, whether by intent or default, increased the school principal's official leverage over his teachers, by giving him the power to approve or reject their professional development opportunities. However, by formalizing a previously informal process of professional feedback with his teachers, the state restricted his ability to get his teachers to improve in certain areas. It has made the principal feel more constrained, less powerful.

School choice researchers have not generally taken up this point, focusing instead only on the effects of school choice on the institutional aspects of bureaucratic control, whether or not school choice makes public school principals more structurally autonomous. It may matter just as much whether or not school choice makes school principals *feel* more autonomous: whether choice opens or closes the informal channels of feedback and control that they use on a daily basis, as well as how it affects the social and informational networks in which they operate and in which they create and re-create this power.

Nor have researchers sufficiently explored the extent to which bureaucratic responsiveness is a construct within the larger context of preexisting institutions and structures. One cannot simply wave the wand of the markets and hope for the best; rather, a much more careful and conservative approach is warranted. Policies are not implemented in isolation. For example, within the agency web discussed in chapter 1, any single actor might change the power and discretion of school principals by changing their power relations with other actors. Any action by any one of these actors can simultaneously empower and disempower principals, because that act affects multiple actors and interconnected relationships. Bureaucratic discretion can be disempowering if increased discretion means that resources will have to be spent to maintain or fix the other relationships affected by the new policy. School choice policies may change any or all of these aspects of the autonomy perceived and exercised by public school principals.

Any positive changes brought about as a result of customer attentiveness within the public schools by choice policies might be limited by the actions of, or inertia within, the larger educational bureaucracy. The effect of the New Jersey State Board of Education's attempts to increase control over the teachers' PIP programs was—according to the PTA representative at the meeting—potentially destructive for her ability to influence the school teachers and, most important, completely beyond this principal's control. Of course state boards of education are only one of the actors involved in the public school bureaucracy. Many other actors and interests are involved, and school choice policies may interact with the powers of these groups in ways that may or may not have been intended.

In spite of the constraints placed on public school principals in hiring and evaluating teachers, the small group of principals in my study believed that their vision of quality education could not be translated into reality without their teachers. That principal and teacher influence are connected does not necessarily imply that the interests of principals and teachers are always in alignment. They were quite often not in alignment, even in the small group of administrators that I studied. However, each of the principals indicated to me that the teachers are critical to implementing their visions of educational quality.

"I've never realized how powerful teachers can be," the least experienced principal in my study tells me, echoing comments by his more experienced colleagues. His school, since it is one of the receiving schools for New Jersey's pilot interdistrict public choice program, is gaining students and resources, and he is eager to increase his school's visibility. He sees these efforts as closely connected to those of coordinating and improving the performance of his teaching staff. Though he has far less influence in hiring, rewarding, and firing his teachers than managers in business and industry, he feels that the quality of his product is just as closely connected with his ability to manage his team as any private manager.

"They [the teachers] can make or break any initiative I have in mind," he continues. "If they're not behind me, they can negatively influence the students, who influence their parents. In my first year, I learned two things. Never take away a photocopier. And don't change the grading system in your first year." He did both and regretted both. The "buy-in" of the teachers is key, he reports, especially of an influential subset of these teachers. "You've got to get those teachers who have the biggest following, the power brokers. I have department chairs. I try to run as much by them as I can. It sometimes gets hot . . . but at least I know the pulse."

Each of the principals I observed regarded the local school boards as powerful or potentially powerful. School boards typically grant tenure to principals and hire and fire their bosses, the district superintendents. "I had a teacher with a board member's child in her class," one of the principals told me, "and the board member was not happy. If you've got a board that undermines you, collect your paycheck and go home."

The main issue with the school boards, from the point of view of the principals, is that board members are responsible to a constituency whose boundaries may only partially overlap with those of the principals' own constituencies. Some of the landowners and business owners who often support or become school board members may not want to see property taxes increased to pay for an educational vision. The principals I studied felt that school boards acted most effectively when they did so through the district superintendent, though several reported that board members did not always do so. More than one expressed a desire for board membership training courses, to teach them how the educational system works, or is supposed to work, and to instruct board members that it is not acceptable to ask to use the school's swimming pool for a child's birthday party.

The pathways of influence on the part of state boards of education described by the public school principals whom I observed were highly correlated with the socioeconomic status of the district. Principals in the poorest schools I studied, the ones that received most of their money from the state, felt that the main power of the state boards resided in their control over the statewide achievement tests (poor districts often underperformed and were threatened by sanction). The data obtained by New Jersey assessment measures compare schools and districts, not on what they add to the achievement of their students, but on what level of achievement students demonstrate. It is not a value-added measure. Principals of these schools, therefore, felt more immediately constrained by the state due to the scores of their students on these tests than their wealthier counterparts.

If New Jersey were to adopt a value-added assessment system, however—one that compares schools and districts based on the year-to-year gains made by their students—then it might produce a very different incentive structure. In that case, school districts under choice might compete for kids from the central cities, not just the academic or athletic stars, but any student who might apply him- or herself, in the hopes of raising the value-added assessment scores of the district. When you are a principal in a wealthy district with kids on their way to selective colleges, year-over-year percentile gains might be hard to achieve without reaching out to the less affluent community.

As it is now, however, public school principals in poor urban districts know that the test results are more critical to their relationship with the state than they are in wealthy achievement-oriented ones. "I know my kids have to pass the ESPA," a principal in a low-income district remarked. "The [state-developed] performance standards are what ties the school to the state. For us, those standards are a challenge. For urban districts like us, the only game in town is the testing." A principal in another urban district in another part of the state agreed: "The tests drive my curriculum."

For wealthier districts, state-devised tests may matter but only indirectly. Principals in the wealthier districts that I studied were not directly

concerned with the state's influence. The principal in the wealthier district was more sanguine toward the state professional development monitoring program with which I began this chapter.

> It's a shot across the bow. They want to see how the political pieces fall. That's how the state department works. Right now, they're talking about changing the graduation requirements. Nobody, not the superintendent, the other principals, is worried. It's not going to happen.

The point is not that state departments are ineffective in constraining wealthy districts, only that they do so in a mediated way, through the parents. The difference is that the state tests make wealthier districts more accountable to their parents and potential parents. There is little likelihood that a wealthy district will come under state control under any assessment system that is not value added. Rather, test scores act as prices, which potential and existing homeowners, those with sufficient resources to live in these districts, compare in selecting or valuing their home. They are badges, important ones, but their influence works through the parents, not the state.

There are a few things that these conversations might suggest to researchers of the effects of school choice on the relationship between the public and the public schools. The first is that choice policies are not the only game in town. One interesting aspect of educational reform in the United States today is that we are simultaneously implementing the somewhat radically decentralizing reforms of school choice and the oddly—from the perspective of a Republican administration—centralizing reforms of high-stakes testing under the No Child Left Behind Act. This complex dynamic deserves the attention of educational policy researchers but is far beyond the scope of this study.[13] More central to my analysis is the potential that educational reforms might impact resource-rich and resource-poor communities differentially.

The Politics of Scarcity and the Politics of Possibility

I am at a Program Committee meeting in the wealthiest of my six districts, the one whose students had the European disco adventure. The Program Committee is a subcommittee of the local school board. Several board members are in attendance, along with the mayor, two of the district's

principals, the district superintendent, assistant superintendent, parents, and a reporter for the local newspaper. The committee has no real power, the principal tells me after the meeting, but it is "a good sounding board." The principal has asked several of his teachers to come to the meeting to comment on the primary agenda item for the meeting: the district's advanced placement (AP) courses. These are classes designed to replicate introductory college-level courses and to prepare students for the AP tests, which allow advanced students to place out of introductory college courses in college and move right into the higher-level classes.

The principal and his teachers feel that too many students are taking AP courses, primarily because their parents are pushing students into these classes when they are not prepared, pressuring the teachers and principal to accept their students, and hoping for a competitive advantage in college admissions. One of the teachers in the school presents some data on the number of students taking AP courses, which has risen sharply, and the subsequent grades of these students, which have been falling. "Too many kids are in AP," she says. "Some of them are not prepared and have to move back out." Last year, teachers recommended fifty-seven students for the AP courses. More than a hundred eventually enrolled.

One of the school board members interrupts the teacher. He tells her that she needs to use regression techniques to better analyze these data, to be better prepared when parents complain, which they inevitably will: "If someone wants [their student] to take a course, and you want to discourage them, then you need the data." He suggests getting AP math and statistics students to crunch the data. "We might even be able to get some money from the [school] board for this."

The principal in my study joins the conversation in support of his teacher's proposal. "The bottom line," he says, turning to another—I later find out, more sympathetic—school board member, "is that we're asking for support from the administration to say 'No.'"

The skeptical board member pushes the data issue again. "We need the data," he says, "to be able to say for sure that it doesn't work for some kids, as opposed to we'd like to close this off because we have a feeling about it." Another board member joins the discussion, turning to the principal. "You might be able to frame this to lobby for more money for guidance counselors. You have to be bold with your plugs."

Later, in his office, the principal tells me that he is reasonably pleased with how things turned out, as he wasn't expecting much. His objective was to test the waters before going to the full board. "We walked out with another task," he tells me. Of the local school board members, he says, "I've been here before. This is a very educated board. They can really take

you out to left field. We'll come up with a [school] policy statement. When a parent doesn't support our decision, we'll pull it out."

There is another, less controversial, issue about advanced placement on the agenda at the meeting. An "anonymous benefactor" in the community offered to purchase, for the high school, on-line AP test preparation software for the students. The principal has done some calculations and placed the value of the offer at just under nine thousand dollars. He feels that the school is already doing quite a bit of test preparation and is cautious about accepting curricular gifts. He wants to decline the offer, and only brought it to the Program Committee's attention to be "prudent."

One of the board members agrees. She notes that another member of the community has offered to pay to set up a gun safety course at the high school. The principal says he will decline the test preparation offer.

> These things can get very cloudy when someone is holding a fistful of money and saying "Do this right now." We're going to be, in the next several years, approached by people with very different philosophies.

One month later I am attending a site-based decision committee in one of the poorest districts in New Jersey. It is a school-based committee, aimed at bringing the principal, teachers, parents, and students together to improve the quality of education along with parental involvement with school policies. The fifth item on the agenda for this evening is one of celebration. Each of the classrooms in the school will finally have a computer.

After the meeting, the principal tells me that, though he is pleased about the computers, the resource inequalities between New Jersey school districts are shameful. I ask him about the parents at these site-based decision meetings, why I always see the same two or three faces in the parent group, and if these few parents are actually representative of his parent community. They are not representative, he tells me, but an affluent, and usually nonminority, subset of the community. The principal tells me that he has worked in wealthier communities, and he notices very clearly that the parents in this district are less attentive and active.

> Parents always have the power. It's a question of "Do they use that power?" Parents are a very integral part of keeping schools on their toes. That's one reason [the wealthy districts] have such good schools. It's not that the urban parents care less than the parents in [these districts]. Our parents are too preoccupied with survival to be confident, capable consumers.

For him, parent involvement often means job requests. His school is a potential source of reliable employment and good benefits in a neighborhood with few other options. Though he feels that his parents are, on average, less involved than those in wealthier communities, his parents are not homogenous in the expression of their political voices. He is very concerned about the loss of his activist parents to the local charter school.

> The most valuable parents are those with different perspectives. The more divergent views you have . . . What's the old saying, "If both agree, one is not needed"? It keeps everybody honest. What fills that vacuum when they leave for the charters? I don't think that it gets filled. Who is involved in [the wealthy districts]? The stay-at-home well-educated mothers. We don't have many of those in our district. These parents can be an effective counterweight to the board. They're the same parents that vote . . . the old squeaky wheel.

This is not to say that the exercise of parental voice is always a good thing. Offers of help can be constraining, and parental involvement may detract from rather than add to the quality of the educational services. Albert Hirschman commented on this potential, noting that "the disconnected customers or members could become so harassing that their protests would at some point hinder rather than help whatever efforts at recovery are undertaken."[14]

It seems more realistic to think of the relationship between the benefits of political activism on the part of parents and the volume of their voices as curvilinear. When there isn't much participation in a school or district, more is better. If you are the principal in a low-income district where parental involvement is minimal, and it consists of job requests, you might welcome parental interest in volunteering at school. When there is so much participation that the principal feels constrained by parent involvement, to the point where his students may not be taking the courses that they should, then more and louder parents probably will not help the educational services very much. A principal in a middle-class district, though generally positive on his parental involvement, acknowledges that there can be too much of a good thing: "I have two hundred and fifty conversations a day. My biggest fear is that all of my parents get email access next year. That's a summer project I'm working on."

These conversations and observations suggest that the consequences of losing activist parents to a charter school or private school might be equally dependent on the levels of voice in the community. In participation-rich districts, the loss of a few noisy parents to the local charter school might actually be beneficial, freeing up the principal's time and burdening the charter school with their involvement. The problem, though, is that the volume of voice—the level of participation—is neither randomly nor uniformly distributed. High-income communities have lots of voice, low-income communities not so much. Therefore, in spite of efforts to target choice programs at low-income and minority communities, school choice might hit the low-income communities harder, at least in terms of parental participation.

Charter Schools and an Uneven Playing Field

There was a general perception among the principals I studied, even those that benefited from the policy, that the impact of the charter school program was unfair. The principals uniformly felt that the public schools were being asked to respond to the challenges of the charter schools with extra constraints placed on them. "We had to pay the charter schools for their students before we got our money from the state," the principal of the urban school whose district sent more than a million dollars to the charter school that occupied the top floor of his building told me. "They get their halls painted while we're waiting for ours." He feels that state politicians want the charters to succeed, even if it costs his students something in return. In many aspects of the legislation, he is correct. There are different regulations for charter and traditional public schools. Charter schools can more easily exclude students who don't buy in. Perhaps most important, the charters, as a result of their newness, are able to hire younger, cheaper teachers, while almost all of his teachers in this urban school district are at the top of the pay scale.

Most of the money this principal's school receives comes from the state, and, he tells me, at the price of increased oversight and regulation compared to the charter schools. The principal, although very accommodating in general, wouldn't let me bring up my interest in charter school legislation at the first of his school's monthly site-based decision meetings that I attended. "We wouldn't get anything done all night," he warned me. "I was forced to lay off senior teachers. Imagine." He brought up the subject himself, at the second meeting. He was correct. They didn't get anything else done all night.

He was not the only principal to talk about the uneven playing field in the charter school legislation designed by the New Jersey state assembly. "I have to stay in the locked gates of my school yard," another principal told me, "while their kids [those of the local charter] can go where they want. There has been a vast impact," she says, on her urban district, in the shadow of one of the wealthiest areas in New Jersey, which has sent dozens of children to the local charter school. "If one of my teachers goes to the charter school and doesn't like it, I have to take them back." She is considering taking graduate courses in marketing. "In graduate school," she continues, "there wasn't much emphasis on marketing. We can't just sit back and do things as they were. It does make you try to be more progressive. We lost quite a few children. I want to know why."

These conversations suggest an important question to which educational policymakers might want to attend: Are schools of choice—whether they are charter schools or voucher-accepting private schools—advantaged in their ability to respond to their customers? Even if they are, that does not necessarily imply that school choice reforms are "bad." There may be good reasons to support these experiments, even if they are unfair to the traditional public schools. The larger concern is whether any positive educational outcomes observed within the choice options are due to the inherent nature of marketplace competition or to the advantages enjoyed by these marketplace competitors.

Voter Turnout

"Last year," the principal of one of the six schools in this study tells me, "the [budget] referendum failed by three votes. It forced a staff reduction."

He is the least experienced of the principals in the study. His school is an intradistrict public choice pilot school, which singles the school out as a clear beneficiary of New Jersey's school choice experiments, receiving more, not fewer, resources in response to the policy changes that New Jersey has undertaken. He also knows, however, that his school's financial health depends on a poorly attended budget election every spring.

"Over the past few years," he tells me, "we've consistently had our budget defeated." Until recently, his was an agricultural district. Farmers, landowners, and business interests, he says, had dominated the school board. They resisted the higher property taxes that come with larger district budget requests.

> You would think that the parents would be more involved, more intimately connected with the vote, but that has not happened. But we're getting a lot of parents who work in New York who are starting to say, "Enough is enough." This year the budget [request] has

the support of the PTA. That's their power. Now they have the strength to do that. Parents are taking a proactive stance.

Any public function, I'm trying to get the parents involved in it . . . kaffeeklatsch meetings . . . telling them what we need. You have to do this to survive. A good principal has to be an active, savvy principal. If you are, the parents will cut you a break. Educating and mobilizing parents is what makes the difference between a status quo high school and one that's on the move.

It's a perpetual process of education. The kids are going to grow up. I'm going to have to educate another generation of parents.

It is a week before the budget vote in the district of this same young principal. We are at a parent advisory committee meeting that the principal has scheduled. This principal is legally constrained from making any public statement in support of the annual budget request; however, he has invited several teachers to the meeting, one of whom is a union representative, none of whom are similarly constrained. The union representative talks about how important the vote is, and how close it is likely to be. There is a discussion about how little the voters know about the impact of the vote on the school's performance. One of the parents in the room offers to help the principal get the word out on how important it is for parents to mobilize and vote for the budget requests. The principal politely declines, saying he cannot legally enter the debate.

This year was a good one for passing base budgets in New Jersey. Eighty-eight percent of the budgets put forward passed, the highest approval percentage since officials began keeping statewide records in 1977. New Jersey's commissioner of education attributed the results to a strong economy and stepped-up state aid for districts, which lowered the burden on property taxpayers. Observers also attributed the good fortune to better financial management by districts and smarter use of taxpayer dollars.[15]

Special ballot questions requesting onetime revenue enhancements also did well, with seventy-nine requests to exceed the New Jersey's 3 percent budget cap to undertake a major capital investment, program overhaul, or hiring initiative. Fifty-four of these special questions sought an increase for renovations, while forty-one sought the increase for increasing and retaining staff. The remainder was for transportation issues and technology and language instruction initiatives. Voter turnout, however, remained low, with less than 13 percent of registered voters participating in the April elections, leading the commissioner of education to renew calls to move the spring elections to the fall to help combat general apathy and the fact that most New Jersey voters do not have school-age children.[16]

The budget vote was mostly positive for the young principal's district. The primary budget request passed in the April election. However, a second question, designed to raise money to avoid having to send the school buses out in shifts, failed. The first class of the fall semester will start at 7:20, which does not make the teachers at all happy, the principal says. "If the first question had failed," the principal tells me, "I would have had to fire six teachers."

> I can't support the budget. What I can do is talk about how important it is to vote. On Election Day, I got on the announcements. We have seniors who are old enough to vote. "This is your first exercise in what it means to be an American," I told them. Get 'em all fired up. I said nothing about making sure the budget passes. Nothing stays in this building. I worded my statement very carefully. Next election, I'm going to do more advertising.

Turnout is critically important to this principal, as he knows that a very small number of the district's registered voters can shape his school's policy in significant ways. Getting support for the budget presents this principal with a traditional collective action problem and the need for political mobilization.[17] Any potential effects on citizens' political behaviors outside of the school and classroom arising from increasing choices within or beyond the public sphere, therefore, deserve the attention of educational policy researchers.

Conclusions

This chapter began my study of the democratic consequences of school choice in the public sector by observing and interacting with a small group of public school principals. The goal was to expand and clarify what parental involvement means in the current school choice debate, which has tended to rely, as the Milwaukee voucher data show, on very narrow conceptions of what it means for a parent to become involved with his or her children's schools. Even working with a small number of individuals, I learned a great deal about parents, choices, and the public schools.

Public school principals consciously and strategically use their parent communities to achieve their vision for their school. They think parents are important. Parent communities are heterogeneous, both in terms of the activism of parents within a school community and also across different communities. Of particular concern is the relationship between the wealth and level of education within that community and participation by its most active and involved parents. One should be careful not to reify parental involvement, however. Sometimes it can be constraining, particularly if the principal already has a great deal of involvement in his or her school community.

Similarly, one should not overestimate the ability of any choice policy that increases parental involvement to fix everything within the public schools. Parents are only one group of actors in the agency web that principals face, and benefits from becoming more customer-oriented may be blunted, or reversed, by the interests of or inertia created by other actors in the system. The importance of participation, and of principals' attempts to influence and use that participation, extends beyond the school and is necessary to securing financial resources for the school, in terms of public support for the budget and individual support for program initiatives. With these lessons in mind, I now turn to an original survey of public and charter school principals in Minnesota to begin to explore the consequences of charter schools for principals and parents within the schools themselves, taking a more careful and more informed look at the effects of charter school reforms on principals' attempts to reach out to their parent communities and the parental responses to these efforts.

4 | Charter Schools, Parental Involvement, and the Public School Principalship

If we are still around next year.

—Minnesota charter school principal, writing in a response to the question "Which of the following measures of school performance most effectively measure your leadership as principal of your school?"

FROM ITS HUMBLE BEGINNINGS as an idea scribbled on a cocktail napkin, the charter school movement has emerged as one of the most promising school choice reforms around. There are now roughly three thousand charter schools operating in forty-one states. Unlike current voucher programs, charter schools do not involve spending public money on private institutions and do not, therefore, raise as many alarms in policy debates. Like voucher programs, however, charter schools have yet to prove that they provide unambiguous benefits for the students who enroll in them. There has been no systematic research demonstrating that students in charter schools learn more than students in traditional public schools. In fact, a few recent studies have challenged some of the academic promise of charter schools.[1] A review of studies of the achievement effects of charter schools concludes that there is not yet a conclusion to be drawn. Research paints a mixed picture, even among the higher-quality studies, and there are as yet unexplained differences between achievement effects across states.[2]

For opponents, these results suggest that charter schools may not be worth the effort given the risks that they pose to traditional public schools. For advocates, the lack of data supporting significant achievement gains is due mainly to the fact that charter schools often serve student populations with traditionally low academic performance. Comparing test scores of charter schools and noncharter schools, therefore, may not be particularly instructive. In addition, advocates point out that parents of students in charter schools report high levels of satisfaction. Many charter schools are quite new, and there has not been enough time to collect a sufficient amount of data, especially given the challenges charter schools face in the first years of their operation.[3] Part of the problem—and one that cannot ever be totally remedied—is the lack of a counterfactual. Researchers cannot know how well a given student would have done had he or she not enrolled in a charter school.

Like voucher programs, however, charter schools were never only about the students who attend them. Rather, the hope has always been that charter schools will spur innovation and change through competition, driving traditional public schools to improve their services in response. By turning parents into customers, the argument goes, public schools will become more customer oriented. With more than 90 percent of K–12 students in the United States still attending a traditional public school (as opposed to 1 percent attending charter schools), any widespread benefits from charter schools must be grounded in the positive effects they have on noncharter schools.[4]

In chapter 1, I presented two challenges to the possibility of better public schools through choice and asserted that these challenges need to be kept separate for a fair and thorough treatment of the problem: Choice may not make for more customer-oriented bureaucracies, and, if it does, it may cause other democratic consequences that undermine or offset these benefits. It has not been clearly demonstrated that charter schools—or any other school choice reforms for that matter—pass even the first narrow responsiveness test.

The few studies that have been conducted on the effects of charter schools and other public choice policies on governance and leadership within the public schools have found the public sector's response to be at best modest and incremental,[5] often largely symbolic,[6] and mediated by school characteristics and culture.[7] The lack of evidence confirming large-scale systematic responses to charter schools and other forms of public choice does not necessarily imply that structural reforms will never happen. It suggests mostly that we do not understand the process of bureaucratic response to marketplace reforms very well. Given the theoretical weight carried by citizen-choosers in the market model of school reform, and the impact of these reforms on people's lives, however, an empirical and theoretical treatment of charter schools and their effects on the responsiveness of school principals to their parent community seems worthwhile.

Perhaps most researchers have been looking too far down the causal chain for effects of programs that are still new, in that these studies have focused on the end product, the actual services provided by and the day-to-day operation of the public schools. My goal in this chapter is to look at the bureaucratic reinvigoration side of choice and attempt to answer the question of whether charter schools produce a more customer-focused principalship—within the charters and noncharters—and whether these bureaucratic changes are associated with increased involvement of parents in the decision-making processes of their schools. Any larger systematic benefits must be predicated on an affirmative answer to the question of whether charter schools improve the public school principalship.

Surprisingly, all but a few school choice researchers have skipped over empirical investigations of these crucial, though largely perceptual, first steps in the responsiveness chain, though it is a prerequisite to the larger institutional changes for which researchers have been looking. There is some preliminary evidence that public school principals are becoming more aware of their parent communities as a result of charter school reforms. In detailed case studies of five urban school districts with a large presence of charter schools, the "sound of parent footsteps heading to charter schools is being heard at the school level."[8] Though most of the evidence that we do have is based on a relatively small number of interviews, which precludes large-sample statistical tests, it is important because it stresses the need to understand the larger political effects of educational reforms in context and offers guidance for larger-sample studies, like the one conducted in this chapter. There is also some preliminary evidence that leadership within charter schools is different and better than within their noncharter counterparts. After interviewing officials with one hundred and fifty charter schools in six states, researchers concluded that "charter school leaders think much about what parents want for their children and try to deliver it."[9] These efforts are made more challenging, however, by the ability of parents to leave the charter schools and return to their assigned public schools.

There are, however, also causes for worry. The authors of a study of the effects of charter schools on social capital among parents in Washington, DC, found that, though charter school parents began the school year with a richer stock of social capital than non–charter school parents, these differences appear to fade over the course of the school year, with charter school parents ending the school year with less trust in government than noncharter schools.[10] In addition, any temporary benefits that did accrue to charter school parents were not observed in broader political participation outside of their particular building.[11]

Prior to concluding that the democratic consequences of charter schools are either nonexistent or destructive, however, it is important to note that the parental side of the equation is only half of the story; it needs also to be understood in terms of the bureaucratic responses to this involvement. That is the goal of this chapter. By examining patterns of leadership, outreach, and parental involvement within the public schools—charter and noncharter alike—I look for the footprints of changes in parental participation within the public schools and at the responses of school principals to these perceived changes. In this way, I hope to link the various charter school studies in order to present a more complex, but understandable pattern of what exactly is happening within the charter schools and what is happening to the traditional public schools in response to their presence.

Charter Schools and Principals' Perceptions of Parental Influence

The data for this chapter come from the Minnesota Schools Survey, a mailed survey that I conducted during November and December 2003.[12] Survey questionnaires were sent to 1,434 public and charter school principals in Minnesota. When an individual principal was responsible for more than one school, a survey was sent to only one of the schools. The response rate was very high, with slightly less than 70 percent of those principals surveyed responding during the study period. A smaller percentage of charter school principals responded to the survey, primarily because charter schools are more likely to have one principal overseeing separate "schools" within the same building, and because many Minnesota charter schools are run by teams.

I focus on the effects of Minnesota's charter schools on leadership, outreach, and parental involvement in charter schools as well as traditional public schools. The analysis is based on a comparison of principals' views of their own leadership and parental response to that leadership according to the status of the school—that is, whether the school is a charter school, a traditional public school located in a district where charter schools operate, or a traditional public school located in a district where no charter schools are in operation. This approach makes it possible to look for unique patterns in leadership, outreach, and parental response not only in charter schools, but also in those traditional public schools that face competition or potential competition from them.[13]

The first step in unraveling the complex relationship of charter schools, principals, and their parents is to address the perceptual side of the equation, to examine if charter schools are having an effect on how important principals think parents are. Figure 4.1 presents a condensed summary of principals' evaluations of what effect parental involvement has on their own influence across five school policy areas: setting performance standards, establishing the curriculum, hiring teachers, evaluating teachers, and setting discipline policy at the school. In this figure, principals' perceptions are based on a five-point scale, where a score of 1 indicates that parental involvement limits the principal's influence "very much," and a score of 5 indicates that the principal perceives that parental involvement enhances his or her own influence "very much." While the principals view parental involvement as generally influence enhancing, there are differences between the school policy areas. Parental involvement is considered most useful in those areas of school policy that more directly affect the standards toward which students should aspire, the curriculum that serves to get them there, and the discipline policy that keeps them focused on that effort.

To study the relationship between charter schools and parental influence in a way that controls for the many other factors that affect influence, it is necessary to construct a model of influence in the presence of school choice. A variant of this basic model will be used throughout the analysis of this chapter, with changes only in the dependent variables of

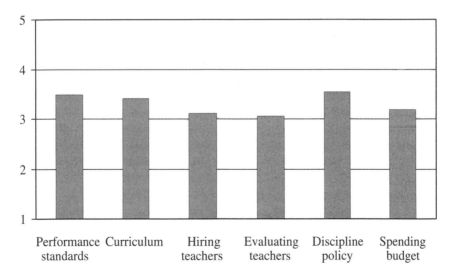

FIG. 4.1.   The effects of parental involvement on principals' influence. Each variable is coded as 1 "limits very much," 2 "limits somewhat," 3 "has no effect," 4 "enhances somewhat," and 5 "enhances very much." (Data from 2003 Minnesota Schools Survey.)

interest. Given what we know about the significant effects on student achievement of the principal's leadership characteristics,[14] community characteristics,[15] and school characteristics,[16] each of the models in this chapter includes a set of professionalism variables[17] and a vector of school and community characteristics.[18]

Most important, a variable is included that represents the school's relationship to the state charter school program: whether it is a traditional school operating in a district without charter schools (the reference for the analyses), whether it is a traditional public school with charter schools in operation in the district, or whether it is a charter school itself.[19] Table 4.1 presents a summary of estimates for the effects of the key charter school variables on the relationship between parental involvement and principal influence.[20] In other words, these results allow me to examine if there are any effects from being a charter school or having one in the district on principals' ratings of the effects of parental involvement, while controlling for other things that might affect principals' ratings.

Charter schools are associated with principals viewing parental involvement as more useful across a range of school policies and activities, and these effects appear to be true of both principals in charter schools and

TABLE 4.1.   The Effects of Parental Involvement on Principals' Influence: Summary of Regression Coefficients

	Charter School Operating in the District (1)	School Is a Charter School (2)
Setting performance standards	0.13	0.86***
	(0.09)	(0.21)
Hiring teachers	0.28***	0.99***
	(0.10)	(0.21)
Evaluating teachers	0.19*	0.54**
	(0.10)	(0.22)
Deciding how the budget will be spent	0.26***	0.53**
	(0.10)	(0.21)
N	928	928

Source: Minnesota Schools Survey 2003.

Note: The survey question was worded as follows: "To what extent does parental involvement limit or enhance your influence on the following policy areas at your school?"

Columns 1 and 2 present relevant coeficient estimates from separate ordered probit regression results. Standard error estimates are in parentheses. Full results are presented in appendix B. The dependent variable is coded on a five-point scale indicating the effect of parental involvement on principals' influence in each area. Each variable is coded as 1 "limits very much," 2 "limits somewhat," 3 "has no effect," 4 "enhances somewhat," and 5 "enhances very much." Student demographic data from the Minnesota Department of Education 2003.

*$p < 0.1$;   **$p < .05$;   ***$p < .01$, two-tailed.

principals facing charter schools in their districts. These attitudinal differences are important, because increased customer awareness is not of much use if the customers are not valued for their involvement. These differences are also potentially important in that they also apply to parental involvement that goes beyond traditional volunteering. Both charter school principals and non–charter school principals facing competition are more positive about parental involvement on issues that directly relate to school governance, including personnel and budget issues.

As in the analyses of the Milwaukee data, it is possible to employ simulation techniques to present the results in a more intuitively understandable pattern (table 4.2).[21] It is clear from these simulation results that charter schools are having the beneficial, early-stage, perceptual effects that advocates have hoped for. Principals in charter schools are more likely to see parental involvement as useful. Parental involvement is seen as more useful in setting performance standards, managing the teachers, and spending the budget. These beneficial changes apply to traditional public school principals in charter school districts as well. It should be noted that the confidence intervals surrounding the predicted percentages of both sets of traditional public schools do overlap, which makes sense, given the

TABLE 4.2.　The Effects of Parental Involvement on Principals' Influence: Predictions

	Public School without Charter in District (1)	Charter School Operating in the District (2)	School Is a Charter School (3)
Predicted percentage of principals who will report that parental involvement enhances their influence			
Setting performance	46%	50%	78%
standards	[41–52]	[43–57]	[61–91]
Hiring teachers	16%	23%	48%
	[12–20]	[18–29]	[32–65]
Evaluating teachers	15%	21%	31%
	[12–19]	[16–27]	[17–46]
Deciding how the budget	25%	33%	42%
will be spent	[21–30]	[27–40]	[27–59]

Source: Minnesota Schools Survey 2003. Student demographic data from the Minnesota Department of Education 2003.

Note: Predicted percentages obtained using Clarify (see King, Tomz, and Wittenberg 2000). Confidence intervals (95%) on predicted percentages are in brackets.

uncertainties in making these kinds of simulated predictions and the small number of charter schools. The underlying estimates, however, are statistically significant. These results indicate that charter schools might be able to induce a customer-centered approach on meaningful issues of school governance, and not just by encouraging parents to volunteer time, energy, or cookies.

Getting the Parents Involved

Attitudinal differences, although worth noting, are only truly relevant if they are accompanied by behavioral differences. Beneficial perceptual effects are not of much utility if they do not translate into actual changes in how school principals actually do their jobs. It may not matter, in other words, whether principals are more customer focused or parent friendly if there are no accompanying organizational changes that facilitate greater parental involvement. In order to look for these more substantive effects, I constructed a similar set of models examining the effects of charter schools on how principals choose to allocate their scarcest resource: their time. Principals were asked to report the relative amounts of time they had spent over the past month in seven school policy areas: facilitating achievement of the school's mission, supervising faculty, guiding the development of the curriculum, building relationships with the parent community, maintaining the physical security of students and staff, managing facilities, and completing administrative tasks. Principals were asked to rate time spent on these activities on a five-point scale, with 1 representing "none or almost none" and 5 representing "a great deal."

Figure 4.2 presents the summary responses of principals to these questions. As one might expect, and as John Chubb and Terry Moe discussed, principals report spending more time on administrative tasks than on any of the other school policy areas that they were asked about. Though most of the other policy areas are similar—hovering around "about as much time as other activities"—the parent communities do not appear to be neglected, at least as reported by principals.

Data from the Minnesota Schools Survey also show that the belief that parental involvement is useful is accompanied by increased attention to building relationships with parents, which is brought about by charter schools and is also accompanied by a more mission-centered leadership style on the part of public school principals, charter and noncharter alike (table 4.3).[22] Both charter school principals and principals of public schools facing competition from charter schools report spending a rela-

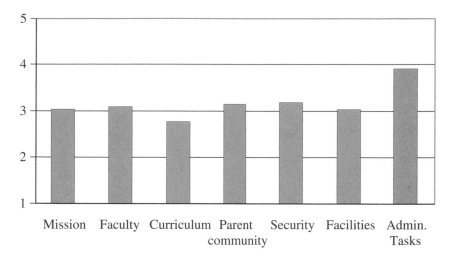

FIG. 4.2. Principals' time spent on activities. Each variable is coded on a five-point scale indicating how much time the principal spent on this activity relative to other activities within the past month. Each variable is coded 1 "none or almost none," 2 "slightly less time than on other activities," 3 "about as much time as other activities," 4 "slightly more time than other activities," and 5 "a great deal of time." (Data from 2003 Minnesota Schools Survey.)

tively higher percentage of their time on achieving the school's mission. These patterns are statistically significant for both groups. Charter school principals also appear to spend more of their time reaching out to their parent communities and less time having to maintain the physical security of students and staff than either of the groups of non–charter public school principals.[23]

Though traditional principals in charter school districts report spending a slightly higher percentage of their time reaching out to parents, these differences are not statistically significant and may very well be due to chance, error, or uncertainty. I cannot conclude, therefore, that the perceptual changes observed in public school principals in charter school districts are associated with greater efforts in outreach. It is also worth noting that the mean scores for the total time spent on all activities do not vary significantly by the type of the school. In other words, it is not merely the case that charter school principals or public school principals in charter school districts feel more time pressures than their counterparts who are not facing charter school competition. Rather, these principals, whether by choice or necessity, spend more time on those aspects of leadership that are associated with achieving the school's mission.

TABLE 4.3.   Charter Schools and the Use of Principals' Time: Predictions

	Public School without Charter in District (1)	Charter School Operating in the District (2)	School Is a Charter School (3)
Predicted percentages of principals who will report having spent "A great deal of time"			
Facilitating achievement	9%	16%	24%
of the school's mission	[7–12]	[12–19]	[19–38]
Supervising faculty	7%	8%	5%
	[4–12]	[6–11]	[2–9]
Guiding development of	6%	5%	8%
the curriculum	[3–11]	[3–7]	[3–15]
Building relationships	10%	11%	22%
with the parent	[8–13]	[8 -15]	[11–34]
community			
Maintaining the physical	12%	10%	5%
security of students and	[9–15]	[7–14]	[2–10]
staff			

Source: Minnesota Schools Survey 2003. Student demographic data from the Minnesota Department of Education 2003.

Note: Predicted percentages obtained using Clarify (see King, Tomz, and Wittenberg 2000). Confidence intervals (95%) on estimated percentages are in brackets.

Valuing parents and focusing on achieving the school's mission, while useful, are only a subset of the desired bureaucratic changes from increasing parental choices in education. Equally if not more important are efforts on the part of school principals to reach out to their parent communities and involve them in significant areas of school policy. Table 4.4 presents summary estimates from models that examine whether schools offer parents the chance to participate in three areas of school policy: as volunteers, in school governance, and in budget decisions, controlling for the same school, community, and principal characteristics as before. Positive and significant estimates indicate that the school is more likely to offer parents a chance to participate, controlling for other variables.[24]

Charter schools are making greater efforts at involving their parent communities in important areas of school decision making; however, it is not possible to state with certainty that these benefits carry over to the traditional public schools. These results confirm that the attitudinal changes toward parental participation are being carried over into action within the charter schools and, perhaps, the traditional public schools in their dis-

TABLE 4.4. Offering Parents a Chance to Participate: Summary of Regression Coefficients

	Charter School Operating in the District (1)	School Is a Charter School (2)
Whether or not principal's school offers parents the opportunity to participate		
As volunteers	0.02	0.12
	(0.24)	(0.39)
In school governance	0.25*	1.34***
	(0.15)	(0.52)
In budget decisions	0.11	1.00***
	(0.13)	(0.37)
N	930	930

Source: Minnesota Schools Survey (2003). Student demographic data from the Minnesota Department of Education 2003.

Note: Columns (1) and (2) present relevant coeficient estimates from separate probit regression results. Standard error estimates are in parentheses. Full results are presented in appendix B. The dependent variable is coded "1" if the opportunity for parents to participate is offered, "0" if not.

$*p < 0.1$; $**p < .05$; $***p < .01$, two-tailed.

tricts. Charter schools are more parent-focused than their more traditional public school counterparts, feel that parents are more influential, and back up those perceptions through increased opportunities for parental involvement. It may be true that traditional public schools in charter school districts are also responding to these competitive pressures, as the coefficient estimates on both involving parents in school governance and budget decisions are positive, and the estimates on school governance suggest the possibility.

The lessons from New Jersey are likely useful here, in that traditional public school principals, however well-intended, have many structural brakes on their ability to produce positive changes in the services that their schools provide. Incrementalism may be as much a fact of life in the politics within the schools as it is surrounding them.[25] The evidence presented so far offers much to be optimistic about in evaluating the bureaucratic consequences of Minnesota's charter school reforms. It appears that charter schools are associated with more mission-focused and customer-friendly public institutions, both at the charter schools themselves and at non–charter public schools facing competition from charter schools.

Charter Schools and Parental Participation

The final piece of the puzzle involves the actual parental responses to what appear to be significant outreach efforts on the part of charter school principals. Table 4.5 presents predicted probabilities obtained from two groups of models.[26] The first explores the relationship between charter schools and the level of parental involvement in those schools that do offer parents the chance to participate as volunteers or in school governance and the budgeting process. Higher coefficient estimates indicate that more parents are participating in the opportunities presented to them. The second model explores the overall trend in participation in the given schools,

TABLE 4.5.   The Level of Parental Participation: Predicted Percentages

	Public School without Charter in District (1)	Charter School Operating in the District (2)	School Is a Charter School (3)
Predicted percentages of principals who will report that *few* of their parents are participating			
As volunteers	30%	28%	19%
	[25–35]	[22–35]	[9–33]
In school governance	72%	77%	50%
	[66–77]	[70–84]	[31–66]
In budget decisions	83%	82%	61%
	[79–88]	[75–88]	[42–80]
Predicted percentages of principals who will report that parental involvement is			
Decreasing significantly	2%	3%	0.6%
	[2–4]	[2–5]	[0.01–2]
Decreasing slightly	9%	11%	4%
	[7–12]	[8–15]	[1–7]
Increasing slightly	39%	36%	50%
	[36–47]	[31–42]	[43–55]
Increasing significantly	6%	5%	17%
	[5–9]	[4–8]	[9–30]

Source: Minnesota Schools Survey 2003. Student demographic data from the Minnesota Department of Education 2003.

Note: Predicted percentages obtained using Clarify (see King, Tomz, and Wittenberg 2000). Confidence intervals (95%) on predicted percentages are in brackets.

with positive coefficient estimates indicating a trend toward more participation.

The efforts of charter school principals to reach out to and involve their parent communities appear to be paying off. Charter school principals are enjoying higher levels of parental involvement and a positive trend in participation. These findings are statistically significant in meaningful aspects of school policy, namely, in governing the school and making budget decisions. Charter school principals also report significant differences in the trend line of parental participation, suggesting that the principals may see even more participatory benefit in the years to come.

Although charter schools appear to be enjoying an increased level of parental participation, traditional public school principals in charter districts are seeing a different picture. In spite of increased efforts on the part of these school leaders to be attentive to their parents, it does not appear that there are any gains in the level of parental involvement. In fact, these principals report a slightly worse picture than their counterparts in non–charter school districts, though these differences are not statistically significant. The worry is that Minnesota's traditional public schools in charter school districts are reporting the same or lower levels of parental involvement because of the departure of more active and involved parents, in spite of the fact that they are more attentive of and may possibly be making more efforts to involve their parent communities. This is a type of potential resource drain that has not been discussed in the charter school literature; however, it could potentially have serious implications for individual public schools. It is possible that the gains in parental participation observed in the charter schools might, in part, be coming about because some of the most active parents are being siphoned off from non–charter public schools in the same districts, and that the processes of parental skimming that I observed in the Milwaukee voucher program are happening in charter schools as well, a pattern that would be consistent with the theoretical framework developed in chapter 1. More evidence is needed on this crucial point.

Conclusions

The evidence from the Minnesota Schools Survey offers many reasons to be hopeful about the beneficial effects of charter schools and the level of parental involvement within the charters, but it paints a more complicated picture of the larger, systemic benefits and costs of charter schools than has currently been discussed in the literature. Minnesota's charter schools are having positive effects, both on the charter schools themselves and on traditional public schools facing competition from the charter schools. These reforms appear to be accompanied by an increased sense of customer awareness on the part of public school principals, as well as increased efforts to nurture the parent community as a valuable resource in the educational enterprise. It is, therefore, premature to claim that charter schools are not having a positive impact on the public school system, even though achievement gains have not been demonstrated in a systematic way.

Customer responsiveness, however, is a necessary but insufficient condition for the creation of effective schools. Albert Hirschman suggested that there might be an "impulse toward an improvement" on the part of public school administrators; however, he also cautioned that such an impulse would not necessarily lead to more responsive schools if an active subset of parents was more likely to exit from the public schools.[27] That my results concur with the predictions of the dominant theoretical model—Chubb and Moe's institutional determinism—speaks to the robustness of both the findings and the authors' institutionalist framework. The distinguishing question, however, from the point of view of Chubb and Moe's hypothesis and that which Hirschman develops in *Exit, Voice, and Loyalty,* is the behavior of the customers themselves. No other group is expected, a priori, to change its composition in response to school choice except the parents themselves. Of course, individual school principals, administrators, and board members may enter or leave the picture in response to school choice; however, school choice policies are predicated on the assumption of a public school parent community whose composition changes as a result of these reforms. Some parents leave.

The evidence presented here indicates that those parents who do leave traditional public schools are welcomed by their charter schools and may very well be learning new skills of participation that they did not learn in the traditional public schools. The reports of parental involvement by charter school principals are consistent with the surveys of parental activity in the Milwaukee voucher program, lending more support to the existence of an underlying social capital–building dynamic arising from the exercise of individual choices in a public system.

Charter schools offer clear advantages over voucher programs, over and above any concerns about providing public monies for religious instruction in the private voucher programs. The difference between voucher programs and charter schools is not just the effect that choosing has on parents, but on the larger consequences for the communities from this exit and its effects. Both charters and vouchers appear to be associated involved parents have left a traditional public school for a charter school, then it becomes more difficult to imagine who exactly is going to put pressure on the public schools to improve and change or who is going to fight for them.

The evidence from the Minnesota Schools Survey does not suggest that any potential school-level costs of charters would outweigh the community-level benefits, only that charters, by themselves, are likely not a panacea for the problems of traditional public schools.[30] Even if school principals in traditional public schools feel compelled to respond to their parent community as a result of charter schools—and these data suggest that they will—meaningful changes in educational services will depend just as crucially on the autonomy of school officials, the preferences of the remaining customers in comparison to their departing counterparts, the coherence of these preferences, and the power of their expression. That traditional public school principals will feel the need to listen to their customers under choice is a point that these data support. However, it may not matter if they are listening, or if they feel like they have to listen, if there is nobody speaking loudly enough for them to hear.

with social capital building, likely brought about, in part, because efforts on the part of voucher-accepting and charter schools to increa their level of parental participation. I cannot say for certain, as I do n have data from voucher principals on their customer outreach efforts. Th expansion of voucher programs currently under way, however, shoul soon make this an empirically tractable question. In addition, in the cas of charters, I am relying on the perceptions of principals about the involvement of their parents rather than on reports from parents them-selves. However, the fact that the charter school principals perceive pat-terns of participation consistent with what I found in the Milwaukee choice program makes me more confident that I am observing the conse-quences of predictable and understandable processes between parents and schools in the presence of exit.

The difference between charters and vouchers is not in the effects that choice has on the parents, but on the sphere in which these benefits are applied. Voucher-accepting parents—at least when public schools are excluded from the program or choose not to participate in it—have left the public system; therefore, it is very difficult to imagine how they are going to make public schooling in their communities better in ways other than through the fear that they strike in the traditional public schools. In the case of charter schools, individual public schools face the potential benefits of competition while—at the same time—the public system benefits from the efforts of the charter schools to reach out and the posi-tive changes that this outreach induces in the parent community.[28]

The benefits of charter schools, however, do not appear to carry over in a transformative way to the traditional public schools. The newly acquired skills that charter school parents have developed will not necessarily be applied within the traditional public schools unless parents leave those charters and return to the public schools, in which case they may very well suffer from the disillusionment that others have observed.[29] The same competition that leads to more customer awareness may not lead to pro-grammatic changes if the traditional school principal does not have the necessary authority and freedom of movement. Moreover, there is a potential for charter schools to siphon off the parents that the traditional public schools need most in their efforts to attend to and involve their community. It is not merely a question of equity, in that it may be unfair to deprive the public schools of active parents. Research clearly supports the beneficial effects of parental involvement on the academic achievement of their children. More central to this analysis, however, is the considera-tion that the most active parents (along with the principals themselves) are going to be the drivers of change within public schools. If the most

5 | The Vote

> Little bands of dedicated souls leave their clear imprint on
> public policy. The duck hunters, the lovers of the national
> parks, the forestry zealots, the disciples of Izaak Walton, and
> many other groups have left their tracks on the statute books.
>
> —*V. O. Key Jr.,* Public Opinion and American Democracy[1]

ON THE SECOND TUESDAY OF EVERY APRIL, 90 percent of New Jersey's
602 school districts must present their base budgets to the voters for
approval or rejection.[2] New Jersey is one of only seven states that allow
citizens this power to weigh in on school budgets, though that power is
limited. School districts that lose on the base budget questions must take
the results of the elections to the local municipal body, which can restore
all or part of the district's budget if it chooses to do so. Districts that fail
to get their budgets approved, however, may be forced to cancel programs
or lay off staff. Most budgets do pass, though there is considerable vari-
ance year to year, ranging from 51 to 88 percent in the past ten years.[3] In
any given election there will be districts presenting their budgets, though
often scaled back, to their voters for the second, third, or even fourth time
in the hopes that they will finally pass.

New Jersey's is a large, fragmented system of educational governance,
characterized by strong local control. The state's 1.3 million students are
distributed over 602 school districts, each with its own school board and
administrative bureaucracy. In New Jersey, local districts assume a 60 percent share in funding for education, while an even fifty-fifty split is the
norm nationwide.[4] Roughly 15 percent of these districts will be bringing
one or more "special questions" to their voters as well: requests by the districts to go over the state's imposed 3 percent cap on yearly increases in
district spending. Questions are usually offered to cover major renovations, teacher recruitment and retention, transportation, or language and
technology initiatives. More than a quarter of these special questions are
repeat attempts. Special questions are more common in wealthy districts
than poor ones. They fare worse in districts with relatively higher property

taxes, and they are associated with higher voter turnout than elections without special questions.[5] Typically, the special questions are evenly divided between requests to undertake a major capital investment or hiring initiative. The small number of remaining questions is usually for transportation issues or technology and language instruction initiatives.

The evidence presented in the previous chapter suggests that charter school reforms will provide substantial benefits to the larger community of public school parent communities, though these benefits may not necessarily accrue to individual traditional public schools. I am, therefore, encouraged by the possibility of bureaucratic benefits from charter schools but somewhat skeptical about the prospect of unambiguous building-level effects from these reforms within the traditional public schools.

I warned readers (chap. 1) that I would be jumping around a bit—though I argued that this was and is necessary to explore something as complex as democracy, bureaucracy, and marketplace reforms in education—and I ask them to follow me back to New Jersey one more time. My goal in this chapter is to extend the exploration of the democratic consequences of charter schools beyond participation in school governance by examining the larger issue of the effects of charter schools on the behaviors of citizens weighing in on public school resources through involvement in and approval of public school budgets. In this chapter, I am venturing outside much of the work in this area. To argue that marketplace reforms can have substantial consequences for participation in local elections—though consistent with the idea of skimming and social capital–building processes that I have explored—takes me beyond research that has been conducted on school choice or political participation.

I focus on the impact of New Jersey's charter school legislation on citizens' participation in and support for school budget referenda. By comparing changes in voter turnout and support for public school budgets between school districts with and without charter schools (controlling for other factors), I test directly whether the introduction of market forces can change democratic political outcomes beyond the narrower world of the schools themselves.

The first point that needs to be made about school budget referenda is that very few citizens will be deciding these outcomes. In a typical year, less than 15 percent of New Jersey's registered voters will participate in the spring budget elections, in spite of the fact that, vote-for-vote, school budget elections present a better chance to influence policy than state and national elections. In close elections with low voter turnout the activities of a small number of citizens can have significant policy consequences. These implications are not lost on those who have a stake in the outcome, such as the principals in districts that have been subject to the what-ifs brought about by the activities of these little bands of voters. On average, roughly 75 percent of budget proposals do pass, though this is not surprising since school districts are strategic in budget-setting behavior.[6]

The fact that a small percentage of New Jersey citizens are involved in setting the district budgets is not surprising and is consistent with more comprehensive studies of voting behavior and political participation.[7] What is interesting about the disproportionate influence exerted by the small group of activists who choose to vote in New Jersey budget elections is just how small this group is and how close the decisions often are. Table 5.1 presents information on New Jersey budget elections that were decided by 1, 5, or 10 percent of the voters in the district for the nearly 3,300 school budget elections in the time frame that I consider, calculated as the absolute value of the difference between the number of yes and no votes divided by the total number of votes cast in that district. Nearly a quarter of the budget elections were decided by a margin of 10 percent or less, and this margin consisted of only 154 votes on average. For the elections decided by a margin of 1 percent or less, the mean number of voters constituting that margin was 18, even though several of these very close elections occurred in districts where more than ten thousand votes were cast.

Charter Schools and Voter Turnout in Budget Referenda

In this chapter, I examine more carefully the relationship between the implementation of New Jersey's charter school legislation and the behavior of its citizens as voters in school budget elections. Using original data collected on the April school budget elections in New Jersey from 1996 to 2002, I focus on two outcome measures: changes in voter turnout and approval rates of base budget requests.[8] The range was chosen to include

TABLE 5.1. Close Calls in New Jersey School Budget Elections

	Percent of budgets decided by		
	1% of Voters (1)	5% of Voters (2)	10% of Voters (3)
Mean number of votes	2%	13%	24%
this margin represents	18	81	154
Range of total votes cast in these elections	88–10,476	76–12,137	36–14,686

Source: New Jersey April Budget Election Study 2003.

data from prior to the implementation of the charter school legislation. As the first charters opened in the fall of 1997, the first election conducted with charters in operation in any school district in New Jersey was in the spring of 1998.

The first problem with conducting an analysis of the effects of charter schools on voting behavior—in New Jersey or anywhere else—is that the percentage of parents who send their children to charter schools is still very small, and the percentage of districts with charter schools in them is relatively small as well.[9] The second, and more significant, problem is that charter schools are not distributed evenly. Though one can find charter schools in the wealthiest districts, they tend to be found in school districts with lower mean incomes and higher percentages of minority students and families—two characteristics that are associated with less political participation. Controlling for these factors in a regression analysis, though helpful, might not take care of the inherent biases that would result.

Therefore, I created a set of matched pairs of New Jersey school districts, one classified as a host district by the New Jersey Department of Education, the other not classified as such. Status as a host district indicates that the charter school is physically located within the district or that the district's students are considered as resident students and given priority for available slots. I focused on host districts that were part of the first wave of charter schools in New Jersey, which means that they had a charter school opening in 1997, 1998, or 1999. This gives me a tractable number of host districts and the ability to observe voting behavior both before and after the charter school opened.

Conducting this kind of matched-pair analysis runs the dual risks of finding a relationship between charter schools and voting behavior when none exists or not finding a relationship when one does exist, since it is not possible to completely rule out the possibility that any findings I observe are merely artifacts of the selection process. In order to at least reduce these possible biases, I tried to be as thorough as possible in choosing and matching a paired district for each charter school district and come as close as possible to finding matches on those district characteristics that are most likely to affect voting behavior in school budget referenda. In addition, each of the districts is listed, along with its salient characteristics, in appendix C, in case other researchers would like to examine and replicate these results, perhaps with a different set of non–charter school districts. I also include a discussion of the process that I used to arrive at these matched pairs.

Table 5.2 presents summaries of the nine matching variables along with the mean voter turnout in the year before the charter opened in the district.

TABLE 5.2.   Summary of Matched School Districts: Demographic and School
Finance Data

	1990 Population	Black (%)	Hispanic (%)	Asian (%)	College Graduates (%)
Charter school	32,898	20.2	13.3	5.5	33.5
districts	(30,624)	(22.2)	(9.0)	(7.0)	(17.7)
Non–charter	31,197	14.0	16.0	5.4	29.1
school districts	(26,190)	(19.3)	(17.9)	(6.2)	(14.3)

	Senior Citizens (%)	Property Tax Base (per resident)	Property Tax Rate	Percentage of State Aid	Turnout in Year prior to Charter Opening
Charter school	14.0	107.4	2.5	31.2	0.12
districts	(4.7)	(147.5)	(0.6)	(28.9)	(0.03)
Non–charter	13.0	83.2	2.6	34.3	0.13
school districts	(4.8)	(67.6)	(0.6)	(27.2)	(0.05)

Source: New Jersey April Budget Election Study 2003. District demographic data from New Jersey
Legislative District Data Book (1996–2003).

Note: Standard deviations in parentheses. Detailed district comparisons presented in tables A5.2 and
A5.3 of appendix B.

The mean scores are close, but not exactly the same between charter and
non–charter school districts. Given what we know and what we expect
about the relationship between community characteristics and participation in budget elections, some of the differences might bias the results in
favor of finding higher participation in charter school districts, and others
might bias the results in favor of finding no differences or lower turnout
among charter school districts.

The higher property tax base and the higher percentage of college graduates within charter school districts would bias these results in favor of
finding higher voter turnout in these districts. On the other hand, the
higher percentage of state aid in charter school districts might bias the
results in the other direction, since budget elections in these districts will
have a smaller net effect as the state is picking up a higher percentage of
the public school tab. Therefore, in the subsequent empirical analysis, I
paid special attention to the statistical significance of those differences that
might bias any findings in favor of finding higher turnout among charter
school districts: the higher percentages of college-educated residents
within charter school districts and the higher property tax base of those
districts. In any case, all of these variables are incorporated in the regression analyses that follow.

A first cut at examining the relationship between being a charter school district and voter turnout is a simple comparison of turnout between host and no-host districts. Figure 5.1 presents these trends by grouping my matched pairs according to the year of the charter school opening. I then look at the turnout in each group of districts in the years following. It is important to note that the non–charter school districts begin with a higher voter turnout than the charter schools. As I will be looking at turnout in a given year, and not at the gains or losses in turnout over the period of the study, the fact that noncharter districts begin with an 8 percent higher level of turnout will work against finding higher turnout in charter school districts over the course of the study. In general, these simple means indicate a secular decline in turnout that is worse for non–charter school districts than for charter school districts.

It is possible that charter schools are working to stem this secular decline in turnout within this group of districts. However, these simple comparisons combine districts whose charter schools—or whose matched charter school district's charters—opened in different years. In addition, this simple graph does not account for potential correlates to voter turnout, or any differences produced by my matching procedure. In order to examine the relationship between voter turnout and charter schools more systematically, I constructed a regression model of voter turnout that incorporates potential correlates of political participation in school

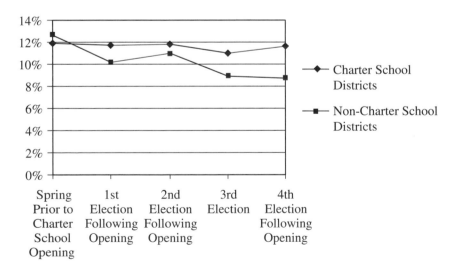

FIG. 5.1. Voter turnout before and after charter school openings. (Data from 2003 New Jersey April Budget Election Study.)

budget elections. The key variable for this analysis is the number of registered voters in a school district divided by the number of votes cast in a given year's spring budget election. Positive and significant coefficient estimates on this key independent variable, therefore, would indicate that districts with charter schools have higher turnout than non–charter school districts, controlling for other possible determinants of turnout.

The model of voter turnout includes a set of special question indicator variables to capture the potential effect of the presence of special questions on the April ballot, as it is reasonable to expect that differences in turnout within a district will be associated with the presence of special questions in the current or previous year. In terms of special questions, we should expect this: Districts that have one this year but not last year should have higher turnout, all else being equal, since requests for large amounts of money usually get voters' attention. Districts that had one in the previous year but not in the current year should expect to see a drop-off in turnout. Districts that propose special questions two years in a row should expect to see increased turnout, since asking voters for extra funds two years in a row might rile the voters up.

As is clear from the results in table 5.3, charter school districts had significantly higher levels of voter turnout than non–charter school districts. The relationship between charter schools and turnout is substantively as well as statistically significant. Given that the mean turnout in these thirty-six districts over the period of the study is 11 percent—all else being equal—charter school districts are associated with a level of voter turnout that is 22 percent higher, hardly a trivial difference. The coefficient estimates on the special question variables indicate an intuitively understandable pattern, following the predictions that logic would suggest. Districts that had a special question only in the current year display higher turnout, relative to districts with no special questions in the current year. Districts that had one or more special questions in both the current and previous years have much higher levels of turnout. Districts that repeatedly turn to their voters for special budget increases do appear to catch the attention of their voters.

The estimates on the district demographic and school finance variables are also consistent with what we know and expect about participation in elections in general and budget referenda in particular, and they also give me some confidence that the differences in charter and non–charter school districts in my set of matched pairs are not driving these results. Two of the district-specific characteristics on which my charter school districts scored higher—the property tax base and the percentage of college graduates—are statistically insignificant in these models. The third—the percentage of

TABLE 5.3.   Charter Schools and Voter Turnout in New Jersey Budget
Referenda

	Effect on Voter Turnout (mean = 11.0) (1)	Standard Deviation (s.d. = 4.9) (2)
Charter school operating in district	2.38***	(0.65)
Special questions on the ballot		
Current year	1.50*	(0.86)
Previous year	–0.88	(0.85)
Current and previous years	3.26***	(0.96)
Property tax base (1,000s)	–0.01	(0.01)
Property tax rate (mills)	–1.19	(0.73)
State aid (%)	–0.05**	(0.03)
Demographic characteristics		
Black (%)	–0.043*	(0.025)
Hispanic (%)	–0.042*	(0.025)
Asian (%)	–0.024	(0.041)
College graduates (%)	–0.034	(0.031)
Senior citizens (%)	0.078	(0.137)
Year indicators (1999 is reference)		
1996	2.57***	(0.93)
1997	2.04**	(0.88)
1998	0.68	(0.99)
2000	–2.05**	(0.92)
2001	–1.50*	(0.89)
2002	–2.05**	(0.94)
Constant	16.95***	(4.16)
N	252	
R^2	0.44	

Source: New Jersey April Budget Election Study 2003.
Note: Column (1) presents coefficient estimates from OLS regression results. Column (2) presents standard error estimates. The dependent variable is the number of votes cast in each budget election divided by the number of registered voters in the district in that year (and multiplied by 100). The key independent variable is coded "1" if the district is a host district for a charter school and the charter school is in operation at the time of the election, "0" otherwise.
*$p < .1$;   **$p < .05$;   ***$p < .01$, two-tailed.

state aid—is accompanied by small effects, given the close percentages in
the matched pairs. Of course, this does not mean that these factors are
irrelevant for voter turnout, only that they may not be driving the results
in this small set of matched New Jersey school districts.

I do not want to overstate the implications of these results, though I do
think that they are intriguing. It is not possible to assert that the charter

schools are causing the observed patterns of participation in districts where charters are implemented, only that there is a correlation between the two. It is possible that there is some other unobserved causative factor that is accounting for the observed differences; however, that factor is likely something that is not a function of the matching process. The most likely counterexplanation is that I am witnessing the effects of a more civic-minded parent community in my charter school districts, responsible for both the higher turnout and the presence of the charter schools themselves. In the absence of surveys of parents in these districts, which I do not have, I cannot rule out this possibility.

However, voter turnout prior to the opening of the charter schools was lower in charter school districts, suggesting that—though there may have been a latent pool of social capital in these districts—the charter schools may have at the very least played a role in awakening this potential. The differences I observed are quite large, and I believe that it is unlikely that civic-mindedness is distributed that unequally between charter and non–charter school districts, differentiated, not by demographic characteristics, but only by the presence of charter schools in those districts. Rather, these results appear to be consistent with the idea that the school-level social capital–building effects that I observed in Minnesota's charter schools do, in fact, extend beyond the school walls. Having found what I believe is limited but useful evidence in support of the relationship between providing citizens with more choices within the public space and participation in the political processes governing these public institutions, I now turn to the relationship between charter schools and approval or rejection of the school budgets on which parents voice their preferences.

Approval and Rejection

In order to examine the relationship between charter schools and budget approval, I constructed a similar set of four models using the same New Jersey voting data as before. The dependent variable for this analysis is a simple dichotomous approval/rejection variable, coded 1 if the budget passed, 0 if it failed. In New Jersey there must be more votes in favor of budget requests than opposed to them in order to pass a budget, as a tie is treated as a failed budget request. All of the explanatory variables are the same as in the voter turnout models, including the key charter school district variable. Table 5.4 presents the coefficient estimates obtained from regression of the budget approval/rejection variable. Table 5.5 presents the estimated probabilities of budget success in the charter and non–charter school districts in the study, obtained using the same simulation methods employed in previous chapters.

The results of the approval models are striking. Voters in charter school districts are less likely to support their districts' requests on base budget elections than non–charter school districts. These estimates on the charter school variable are statistically and substantively significant, as the predicted probability for budget success is just over 15 percent lower in char-

TABLE 5.4.   Charter Schools Budget Success in New Jersey

	Approval of Base Budget (mean = 0.73) (1)	Standard Deviation (s.d. = 0.44) (2)
Charter school operating in district	−0.61**	(0.26)
Special questions on the ballot		
Current year	0.36	(0.37)
Previous year	−0.30	(0.33)
Current and previous years	−0.52	(0.44)
Property tax base (1,000s)	0.0001	(0.001)
Property tax rate (mills)	−0.56**	(0.25)
State aid (%)	−0.003	(0.009)
Demographic characteristics		
Black (%)	0.01	(0.01)
Hispanic (%)	0.001	(0.01)
Asian (%)	−0.07***	(0.02)
College graduates (%)	0.03***	(0.01)
Senior citizens (%)	−0.11***	(0.04)
Year indicators (1999 is reference)		
1996	−0.21	(0.36)
1997	−0.45	(0.20)
1998	−0.46	(0.17)
2000	0.43	(0.24)
2001	−0.17	(0.37)
2002	−0.44	(0.37)
Constant	3.91***	(1.27)
N	252	
Wald chi^2 (19)	41.98	
Prob > chi^2	0.00	

Source: New Jersey April Budget Election Study 2003.

Note: Column (1) presents coefficient estimates from probit regression results. Column (2) presents robust standard error estimates. The dependent variable is coded 1 if the base budget was approved by voters in the district, 0 otherwise. The key independent variable is coded 1 if the district is a host district for a charter school and the charter school is in operation at the time of the election, 0 otherwise.

$*p < .1$; $**p < .05$; $***p < .01$, two-tailed.

TABLE 5.5.   The Presence of Charter Schools and Probabilities of Budget
Success

	Probability of Success		
	Mean (1)	Standard Error (2)	Confidence Interval 95% (3)
Charter school districts	0.67	(0.07)	[0.52–0.79]
Non–charter school districts	0.79	(0.03)	[0.72–0.85]

Source: New Jersey April Budget Election Study 2003.
Note: Probabilities obtained using Clarify (see King, Tomz, and Wittenberg 2000).

ter school districts than non–charter school districts. In addition, the
coefficient estimates on other variables in the model conform to what we
know and expect about budget approval rates. Districts with higher property tax rates are associated with lower approval rates, as are districts with
a higher percentage of senior citizens living in them and those with fewer
college graduates.

These findings are even more striking when one remembers that there
are few reasons based on self-interest alone for charter school parents to
vote down budget requests. Charter school funding comes from the same
kitty as traditional public school funding. Rejecting a district's budget
request will negatively impact the budgets of the charter schools operating
within it.

These results are rather startling, but what do they mean? I see three
possibilities, though I cannot rule any of them in or out. The first possibility is that there is nothing going on at all. Though I have confidence in the
robustness of the associations and the data underlying these results, it is
possible that these results are unique to these data, from one state and
using a small set of matched pairs. More research is probably needed. It is
important to note, however, that other patterns in my results corre-
sponded to what we know and expect, so it is not likely that this is all just
noise. The second possibility is one of disillusionment. Perhaps charter
schools encourage parents and citizens to get involved, and these individuals are not at all happy with their experiences. Other researchers have
found evidence of dashed hopes in the charter school world, and these
results could be a result of this process.

Finally, it is possible that charter school parents are more private-
minded than their traditional public school counterparts. We know that
fund-raising plays a major role in the life of a charter school, particularly
in securing a space. It is possible that charter school parents are turning
inward, devoting themselves to their local bake sales, auctions, and cold
calls at the expense of rallying support for the district's budget request. To

say that voters' preferences can be shaped by the narrow communities of charter school parents is likely not a popular assertion. But it would be consistent with all that I have found so far in this book. Perhaps preferences are not a given.[10] Perhaps gated communities produce narrow minds.

Conclusions

Something important appears to be going on in New Jersey's charter school districts. The expression of citizens' voices in the larger political space may be changing in response to consumer empowerment. The provision of parental choices within the public space appears to alter the expression of citizenship in the democratic control over educational institutions. My results are modest and include only a single state, and one cannot rule out that they are an artifact of the matching process. I can only assert that there do appear to be effects on voting behavior from increased competition, and that researchers would be well advised to keep watching. However, based on the results of the New Jersey voting data and the Minnesota surveys, I can assert with some confidence that charter schools do matter for citizen control over and involvement in public education. The subject of the next, and final, chapter is to reevaluate what I have learned from the analyses in this book and to consider what lessons public policymakers should take away from my findings.

6 | The Personal, the Political, and the Economic

> How unreasonable to expect that the pursuit of business should be itself a culture of the imagination, in breadth and refinement; that it should directly, and not through the money which it supplies, have social service for its animating principle and be conducted as an enterprise in behalf of social organization!
>
> —*John Dewey,* Democracy and Education[1]

> Citizens who are forced to take a part in public affairs must turn from the circle of their private interests and occasionally tear themselves away from self-absorption.
>
> —*Alexis de Tocqueville,* Democracy in America[2]

I BEGAN THIS BOOK WITH A PUZZLE: "What is the connection between equality and liberty in American education?" I argued that a careful and critical exploration of this connection is crucial to our understanding of the likely effects of school choice policies and their larger effects on the functioning of American democracy. The tension between liberty and equality, between politics and markets, is real. It appears to be unavoidable and complicated, but not necessarily hopeless or without the potential for remediation or a careful application of school choice reforms.

By framing the argument in an absolutist sense—one that asks if we should have politics or markets in the provision of education—we miss the possibility for a deeper understanding of the hopes and challenges of introducing market forces in an endeavor that relies on institutions of democratic control for its support and governance. An uncritical faith in either politics or markets is unjustified and reduces effective policy options. I believe that it is more useful to recognize that the tension between equality and liberty is fundamental to American democracy and to use this realization as a basis for providing choices and competition while also securing the political and economic resources necessary to the collective enterprise, thereby helping to minimize the collective costs of individual choice and maximize the individual benefits of competition.

In many ways my story is one of unintended consequences. A reform aimed at improving bureaucratic accountability is going to have substantive consequences on political mobilization and participation in public education. School choice has the powerful potential to make public school principals more responsive to their parents. It makes public school bureaucrats pay attention to their newly empowered parent communities. Exit appears to increase the power of voice. There is also evidence, however, that exit changes the expression of political voice. The louder parents, as Albert Hirschman warned, are likely to be the first to exit, and they appear to become more effective in the process of exit. The effects of these movements and transformations, however, are institutionally and contextually determined. Where parents go matters, both for the schools that they exit to and for the schools that they leave behind. The characteristics of these communities matter as well.

John Chubb and Terry Moe are correct in their argument that democratic political institutions can have deleterious effects on the efficiency of public educational institutions. However, market forces, once unleashed, also have negative consequences for the distribution of political control over the democratic institutions that govern the educational enterprise. The situation, however, is not hopeless. That researchers have found social capital formation to be a dynamic process can be a source of hope or despair for resource-poor communities in the presence of choice, opening up the possibility of reinvigoration in the communities whose active voices have been drained by choice options, particularly if exit is restricted to the public sector.[3] Based on the simultaneous possibilities of destruction and regeneration, I conclude the book by reviewing what I have learned about school choice, bureaucratic responsiveness, and democratic participation and offering some suggestions for educational policy debates and discussions as we move forward from here.

In chapter 2, I examined the effects on political participation brought about by the Milwaukee voucher program and speculated on how the effects of activist skimming and social capital formation are likely to be determined, in part, by the resource levels of those communities. Much of the concern over private school voucher programs is their potential to blur the separation between church and state, in that they provide public funds that can be spent on religious schools. I have not commented on, and have no empirical basis to weigh in on, the constitutional issues involved in private voucher programs. However, I do have evidence to suggest that this is only part of the story with voucher programs, and perhaps not even the larger concern.

By comparing voucher program applicants to a random sample of Milwaukee public school parents, I found that parents who are more active in and involved with their local parent-teacher associations are more likely to apply for vouchers, thereby potentially depriving the existing public schools of their most active and involved parents. By comparing parents who were accepted to or rejected from the Milwaukee voucher program by lottery (after considering the potential biases arising from attrition), I concluded that choice-accepted parents are more likely to increase their membership in, attendance at, and involvement with PTA organizations and sponsored events and activities. Moreover, I found that these beneficial changes in school-level participation in voucher-accepted parents are not independent of levels of parental education within the targeted population. More educated parents appear to benefit more from vouchers than those with less education.

I then turned to a national survey of public, public choice, and private school parents in the United States to begin to explore—or at least speculate on—the comparative consequences to the expression of political voice that might arise from allowing or subsidizing exit within and beyond the public sector. I found evidence to suggest that there may be very different participatory consequences of private and public choice programs, especially in relation to the expression of voice within individual public schools. These consequences are likely to be more significant for public schools within communities that begin with lower levels of parental income and education. I did not examine the potential benefits arising from increased customer responsiveness on the part of public schools that lose customers to private choice options—though I suspect that these benefits do exist—but cautioned that public schools faced with private voucher programs will be attempting to translate any increase in responsiveness into action with a degraded set of parental resources.[4]

In chapter 3, I began my investigations of the effects of public school choice on the public schools—focusing on charter school reforms—with observational studies of a small group of public school principals in New Jersey who were encountering and participating in these reforms. I found that parental involvement in schools is a much more complicated and nuanced thing than simply joining a PTA. The public school principals recognized and tried to use their parent communities as an important resource in their efforts to achieve their visions for their public schools, within the schools or in the securing of financial resources for them. Not all parents, however, figured equally in these attempts. More active and wealthier parents tended to be more useful in these strategic calculations. Wealthier communities had more active parents, and, even in the poorer communities, the subset of activist parents often did not mirror the diversity of the school communities. These principals also taught me that voice is not always a good thing. It can be a distraction from, and not a resource for, educational excellence. Sometimes a public school principal might be happy to "let a few parents go" to the local charter school—though their return upon being dissatisfied with the charter school might present its own problems. The principals in poorer districts, however, were much less sanguine about this potential loss of voice.

In addition, I learned that, for traditional public schools, there are many cooks in the kitchen. To assert that competition, by itself, will produce a more customer-aware public school principalship and simultaneously translate these beneficial perceptual effects into major school policy changes may be too optimistic, ignoring the realities of common agency that traditional public school principals face. This potential, I argued, may blunt even the beneficial effects of charter schools on the operation of the traditional public schools. The hope that charter schools will produce major systemic changes within the traditional public schools that face competition from the charters may be too optimistic in the face of parental skimming and the limiting effects of common agency in the preexisting public bureaucracy.

In chapter 4, I looked for signs of bureaucratic reinvigoration in the presence of choice. I employed an original survey of public school principals in Minnesota—including charter schools, traditional public schools with charter schools in their districts, and those without charter schools in their districts—to explore the consequences of charter school reforms on the perceptions of school principals about parental involvement, their attempts to increase this involvement, and their perceptions of the results of these efforts. I found substantial benefits from charter schools, both in the charter school principals and in those principals in traditional public schools facing competition from them. Charter school principals and those with charter schools operating in their districts appeared to be more customer focused.

I also found that charter school principals were more likely to offer parents a chance to participate in meaningful areas of school policy, specifically in governance and spending the budget within their individual schools. In addition, charter school principals appeared to be enjoying the benefits of the kind of social capital–building effects that I observed in the case of the Milwaukee voucher program, though I offered no evidence for or against the underlying processes, only in the building-level effects that I would expect to observe if this was, in fact, the case. For principals in traditional public schools facing competition from charter schools, however, I found a foggier picture. I did not find systematic evidence that these individuals were able to translate their mission and customer focus into increased opportunities for parents to participate, nor did I find evidence of social capital building within public schools facing competition from charters. In fact, just the reverse may be true. Based on my own and others' observations of the public school response to charter schools, it seems likely that researchers will find evidence of perceptual changes whose good intentions may be blunted by the skimming of active citizens, the multiplicity of actors and interests in the public educational enterprise, or both.

In chapter 5, I turned to the effects of charter schools on the expression of parental voice in the larger sphere of democratic political participation, in this case, in the context of school budget referenda in New Jersey. Though my results might be a result of the district-matching procedures used in the study, and I therefore encouraged other researchers to replicate these findings using their own matching procedures, these preliminary results point to a coherent but troubling pattern. I did find that charter school districts were associated with a higher voter turnout in budget elections. However, I also found evidence that budget approval rates were lower in charter school districts than non–charter school districts. Both of these findings are consistent with a process of withdrawal from the collective enterprise into the cocoon of the charter school, in spite of the fact that charter schools are public in how they are funded.

The evidence that I have presented—and the patterns that have emerged from these admittedly disparate analyses—are consistent with a process of parental sorting and post-sorting transformation brought about by empowering individual choices within education. Those parents with the skills and behaviors that are most able to constrain school performance become overrepresented in choice options, gain in the skills and confidence necessary to nudge their schools to higher performance, and provide the schools that receive these changes with a more active parent community. The aggregation of these individual transformations has the potential to create a troubling redistribution of political and therefore financial resources within and between communities. Based on what I have found, I have two main suggestions for policymakers, one conditioned on the continuation of the current piecemeal reforms under way, the other envisioning a bolder and more comprehensive approach.

1. The debate over school choice needs to begin to account more fully for the institutional complexity of choice reforms and their effects on different parent communities. Specifically, the discussion needs to examine more carefully the effects of public and private choice policies on democratic participation and to do this with an acknowledgment that parental resources are not distributed evenly among and between communities. Charter schools and private school voucher programs are very different educational reforms, and the effects of both are not independent of the communities in which they are implemented. In addition, I believe that researchers need to be more careful to draw distinctions between the building-level and community-level effects of various choice policies.

Based on my analyses, I conclude that educational reforms that facilitate exit to the private sector have a significant potential to damage democratic politics, especially in resource-poor communities. Individual public school principals may not be able compensate for the departure of their most active parents by working harder to get information out to parents, as they may be working with degraded resource and control networks. They will be competing against an energized private sector with their own relatively inactive parent populations. It may be more difficult for the public schools to obtain support for reform initiatives and to motivate citizens to vote for budget requests. This discussion of the effects of institutional design on political mobilization has, up to this point, been missing from the school choice debate. It should not be.

Given these findings it seems reasonable to demand two things of a private voucher program. First, it should unambiguously provide for a better education for the students who enroll in it. Second, a private voucher program should create, or at least not destroy, the political and civic capacity necessary to secure adequate resources for all students, not just those who are lucky enough to enroll in the program.

Reforms, such as charter schools, that facilitate exit within the public sector, however, retain this set of activist parents within the public school system and encourage these and other parents to become more active and involved. Their presence in the educational landscape may encourage the traditional public school principals to become more attentive to their customers. In the case of charter schools, there is reason for optimism and perhaps for concern. Charter school principals value their parents, allow them to be involved in meaningful aspects of school policy, and appear to enjoy greater participation as a result of their efforts.

Within the public school buildings, however, the charter school story is more complicated. Charter school reforms, though useful and preferable to voucher programs, are probably a necessary but insufficient condition for the revitalization of traditional public schools. They will provide the competition necessary to encourage principals in traditional public schools to strive to improve, and they will maintain and probably even nurture the expression of voice within their own walls, but they will probably not be sufficient to solve all of the problems with traditional public schools.

If I were to leave off here, I would have little to offer other than a critique of current policies without providing any unambiguous solutions, leading to an implicit, if unintentional, defense of an untenable status quo. The problem is that the current patchwork of choice reforms is not likely to get us to our ultimate goal: a system that provides excellent education for all children, reforms the educational bureaucracy, and secures a collective commitment to funding excellent schools. While these piecemeal reforms are carried out, we are still going to rely on citizens to pay for, support, and watch over education in this country. Perhaps as important, we cannot forget that not all parents will choose to or be able to exit, unless we instantaneously replace the entire system of traditional public schools with a set of charter schools or similarly promising alternatives. I believe that this possibility is highly unlikely, at least in the short term.

2. If Americans really want outstanding schools for all, and not just a few symbolic lifeboats, then we will have to make difficult choices that will incur opposition from free-marketeers and entrenched political interests. Policymakers in the United States are going to have to wrestle with the much trickier issue of bringing both the advantages of private choice and of collective commitment to public education. If not, then we are going to be presented with a very difficult normative issue, that of letting some parents benefit from choice options while confining the majority to deteriorating public schools while this process of creative destruction works itself out. Therefore—while I argue that charter schools can provide an important alternative to and impetus for bureaucratic transformation within traditional public schools—they are not going to be enough.

I would like, therefore, to conclude this book by considering how we might incorporate the beneficial aspects of the market approach while simultaneously working to secure the collective commitment to educating all children in this country. In order to do that, I would like to return to the tension between liberty and equality, between individual choices and collective commitment, in educational policy.

Liberty, Equality, and Policy

The central idea of this book has been the interaction between the competing forces of individualism and collectivism in civic life. Chubb and

Moe argue for a vision of educational reform based on unleashing individualistic energies to correct for the failures of America's collective commitment to education. I have shown systematic evidence that they were at least partially correct in this view. As I have also shown, however, privileging individual choices undermines that collective commitment and leads to a fragmented polity, offering little hope to all but a lucky few poor parents. The concerns that I have raised in this book are only more problematic given the lack of solid evidence that choice policies are producing any achievement gains for the students who enroll in them. What we are left with is this: We know that we are likely to get heavily class-skewed politics from current choice policies, but we are still highly uncertain that we will see any achievement gains even for those that we let in to the privatized club.[5]

The first step toward a resolution is to realize that it is ridiculous to talk about how we are going to take politics out of education.[6] We can't and we shouldn't. Politics are necessary to securing equality and counteracting the privileging of particularistic interests. The second step is to begin to accept the possibility of having both liberty and equality in education. Policymakers are not used to thinking this way—given that those involved in the school choice debate seem to gravitate to the extremes of the spectrum. Based on what I have learned in this book, however, I think the bolder course of trying to secure both liberty and equality is the only way out of our current dilemma.

We Americans are spending more money on urban education than we ever have—with hardly stellar results—leading some scholars to assert that money does not matter in education.[7] I think that this argument is disingenuous at best. Why would the most successful and wealthy parents spend almost twenty thousand dollars per year on their child's education if money did not matter? Why would parents in the big cities line up to get their kids into the right pre-school or pre-pre-school, even hiring consultants to facilitate the admissions process? Because money does matter in education. It buys excellence, security, connections, and a more effective voice. We parents will do almost anything for our children, even if it means denying opportunities to other kids if that is how it has to be. Critics of increased spending in public education, however, do have one valid point. The money may not have been well spent.[8] Throwing money at an inefficient educational bureaucracy, as many critics of American education have pointed out, has not worked and is likely not to work in the future.

It is all about securing the necessary level of resources, political as well as financial, and using those resources efficiently and for all children.

Many scholars have commented on the disastrous effects of suburban flight on the financial and political bases of the urban school systems.[9] I agree. But I also think that school choice—as we are now doing it, though not necessarily as we can do it—is going to produce the same drain on civic capacity that the flight of middle-class parents from the inner cities did some decades ago. Current choice policies will further fragment poor communities into those that can play the game and those that can't, and those policies are likely to result in the kind of political drain that will make it very hard to maintain even current levels of spending in those communities left behind.

In her book about Social Security, Andrea Louise Campbell pointed to an unanswered mystery in American social policy: In spite of demographic shifts that would seem to favor spending as much or more on children than seniors, it has not happened.[10] Why not? I think the answer is that in Social Security policy we have, as Campbell shows, created a cross-class coalition of seniors allied together in encouraging more spending because of the institutional design of the program. Seniors are in it together. Middle-class seniors fight for benefits in the same policy space as poorer seniors, and the efforts of the most active help secure resources for the more and the less active equally. In education, however, we have fragmented parents into fiscally autonomous school districts and private schools, thereby narrowing the scope of their political involvement. We do not have a national coalition for spending money to educate children because parents, unlike seniors, fight their resource battles within the confines of their school districts and private schools. Any policy reform that continues or exacerbates this fiscal fragmentation will only make the prospect of large-scale increases in education spending even less likely in the future.[11]

But it does not have to be this way. Though politics and markets are presented as opposing forces, this is more a result of how the debate has been framed and shaped than of any inherent incompatibility. "Neither logic nor empirical evidence," according to political scientist Charles Lindblom, "shows the impossibility—even the improbability—of reconciling a real-world market system with a greatly more egalitarian distribution of wealth and income."[12] I have explored the limits of the market and shown how consumer sovereignty is not the ultimate in citizen empowerment.[13] However, markets are not necessarily antithetical to politics either.

What matters is the conscious decision whether to pursue liberty, equality, or both in policy design. These choices are illustrated in table 6.1, which explores the tension inherent in and the consequences resulting

TABLE 6.1.   Pursuing Liberty and Equality in Public Policy

	Lack of Liberty	Liberty
Lack of Equality	Monopoly control No individual choice Some more equal than others	Individual choice Customer orientation Resource inequalities Class-skewed politics
Equality	Monopoly control Lack of individual choice Lack of customer responsiveness Resource equality	Individual choice Customer responsiveness Cross-class coalitions

from facilitating either individual choices or collective commitment in policy design.[14] The distinction between liberty and equality that I present here is a rather stark one, in spite of the fact that there is a long tradition of democratic thought that points out the overlap and necessary connections between liberty and equality as well as the nuances necessary to any definition of either liberty or equality.[15] Nonetheless, discussing liberty and equality as opposing forces—especially in relation to education in the United States—also has a long history and serves to frame much of the current debate.[16] I will accept the narrower, dichotomous framing of the discussion of liberty and equality in order to point out what I see as critical gaps in our current understanding of educational policy.

The first case in this framework is the set of policies that, by design and control, provide neither liberty nor equality in the delivery of services and benefits. Recipients of these policies cannot exercise their individual choices, and they cannot count on the promise of equity and fairness in the provision of services. While it is obvious that few policymakers would argue we should have neither, there are historical examples. Housing policy in the Soviet Union is one that comes to mind. Because supply and prices were set by the state, individuals had few choices in their housing decisions, and the resulting level of housing services was substandard. Some individuals, however, were more equal than others, especially inner party members whose housing was typically of superior quality.[17]

Another option in my framework is to pursue collective commitment in public policy at the expense of individual choice. Equality without liberty frames the basic critique of public education in the United States for those who would increase individual choices within the system. The argument is now familiar: the pursuit of democratic control over education has produced a system that has stifled the beneficial effects of letting individuals choose their schools and forcing schools to compete for customers. Of course, this is an oversimplification. Some parents, especially the wealthy, have always had choices, in paying either private school tuitions or a housing price premium to live in neighborhoods with "good" schools. However, the involvement of democratic control in education has at least reduced funding inequities that would be present without any redistributive policies, but at the cost of monopoly control over educational services and the creation of a set of captive customers.

Contrast that situation with the prospect of pursuing liberty at the expense of equality. The delivery of financial services in the United States might be a good example of liberty without equality. Though there are laws to prevent racial discrimination in banking, one does not find many payday loan centers—with their extraordinarily high interest rates—in the wealthy suburbs. There is nothing in the invisible hand of the markets that is kind and generous to the poor and disenfranchised. In education, these concerns have served as the focus for the empirical work in my book. Liberty without equality produces the Matthew effect, whereby those who have resources get more, and those without, lose what little they have. We may get more responsive bureaucracies, but this responsiveness may come at a considerable democratic cost. This is the greatest worry of those opponents of school choice who fear that voucher programs are little more than the perpetuation or increase of wealth inequality in the United States.

Finally, I would like readers to consider policies that attempt to facilitate both liberty and equality at the same time. The goal, in education, would be to devolve the day-to-day service delivery and governance as far as possible to the individual customers and schools while also evolving the securing of resources for such a system to include the entire polity. Such a system might produce the civic-building effects observed in the case of Social Security and the GI Bill while retaining the bureaucratic benefits of a customer-focused service delivery.[18] However, it is going to take a simultaneous commitment to both liberty and equality to achieve such a vision in education. The path to both liberty and equality does not run through either one alone.

Fully Funded Choice

This is the fundamental question going forward: Can we bind our citizens together in the common purpose of schooling without binding them as individuals to an inefficient and choiceless monopoly system? What we need is at least a state-level commitment to securing resources for poor children in a system that allows for individual choices. What would such a system look like? Ironically, for this last discussion I return once again to Chubb and Moe's *Politics, Markets, and America's Schools.* Though its publication stirred and continues to stir much debate, the one part of their book that received very little attention was their specific plan for an ambitious public choice system.[19] I think that this is unfortunate, as there is much in their plan that is useful and different from ideas for charter schools and voucher systems.[20]

Their plan, broadly outlined, consisted of replacing the current system of education with a new system of public schools. There would be minimal restrictions on what defines a school as public, legitimate, and able to participate. These restrictions would focus on health, safety, and sustaining a nondiscriminatory environment. Public schools would be free to hire, fire, and tenure teachers as they saw fit and to admit, expel, and teach students as they chose to, subject, of course, to maintaining the basic criteria of nondiscriminatory practices.[21] Parents would be free to apply to any school that they chose to, and there would be systems in place to provide transportation and the provision of accurate information about individual schools.

Schools would be financed by collecting the students' individual scholarships, whose values would be set equally for all students in the state and whose funds would be distributed by "parent information centers." The plan is very clear that it would not allow individual parents to supplement their children's scholarships with personal funds or in-kind services, given the concerns with equity. Individual districts, however, would be allowed to supplement their state-set scholarship amounts by raising money within the district, presumably through property tax levies.

My proposal would be to adopt much of what Chubb and Moe suggest, but with a few critical differences. The main flaw of their plan, in my opinion, is that individual school districts would be allowed to raise and spend more than the scholarship amounts dictate. Because of the effects of the participation-feedback loop that I have observed in education, such a system is also likely to suffer the same problems of skimming and inequitable social capital formation and resource distribution that I observed in the case of current voucher programs and charter schools. Parents in wealthy districts would direct much of their political energies into these add-ons and not to the overall level of the scholarship, significantly eroding the resource base of inner city schools and increasing economic inequality in education and beyond.

Individual choice of service providers is not necessarily incompatible with equity in service provision; however, equity of services in education is incompatible with the channeling of political involvement into school districts and gated communities. Citizens and customers must be allowed to compete for services on the same playing field, not before they get there. An educational plan that embraced both liberty and equality might, therefore, look like the following.[22]

- The plan would be enacted at the state level, covering all public schools within the state.
- The property tax would be eliminated as a source of educational funding. It would be replaced by either a state income tax, sales tax, or a combination of the two.
- Choice of residential neighborhood, transportation permitting, would have no impact on how much money was spent on your child's education or on the schools that your child could apply to.
- A per-student scholarship amount would be set by the state, and it would equal for all children. That amount would not vary depending on the financial resources of the student. In other words, there would be no means-testing for scholarships.
- Individual school districts, cities, or towns would not be allowed to supplement these scholarships with any funds, services, or enrichment programs that were not paid for entirely by the scholarships themselves. This would include athletics. All funds raised in this way would be thrown into the collective pot.
- States would be free to add on to scholarship amounts funds associated with children with special needs.
- Private, nonprofit, nonreligious schools and charter schools would be welcomed as public schools in this system, provided they met the minimal requirements.
- Parents would be free to choose any school they wanted to and could gain admission to. Money would be set aside to cover transportation costs.[23]
- Public schools would be able to admit and expel students; to hire, fire, and tenure teachers; and to set their curricula as they saw fit, with minimal restrictions set by the state legislature.

Criticisms of Fully Funded Choice

There will be the same siphoning of the most active parents as I observe in current voucher programs.

At the school level, skimming is likely to occur, leaving some individual schools with less active parents. However, since the program is universal and non–means tested, the more active, educated parents are compelled to fight for scholarship funding in concert with poorer, less educated parents.

If the patterns that we observe with Social Security hold for this type of educational plan, then we can expect all parents to become more politically active, and poorer parents disproportionately so. We might just witness the creation of a cross-class coalition of parents with the same political clout as seniors in the American policy space.

There exists the possibility that the policy will lead to resegregation in American education.

I think that the story is more complicated than that. In the first place, the current system is no model of integration. It is true that nondiscrimination policies can only do so much and may not be able to stop parents from sorting themselves based only on race. However, much of the outrage associated with segregation was the correlation between race and wealth in the United States. I would argue that the reliance on the property tax for educational funding is the single biggest preserver of inequality and segregation in America.

We might just see forms of schooling arise that had tremendous potential to overcome racial segregation. Consider the idea of a public school started on a corporate campus, designed to attract children of workers from all ranks within the organization. I have no doubt that parents would find the prospect of being near their kids, and sharing one commute, attractive. Perhaps the CEOs would still send their children to private schools, but there at least exists a possibility of kids whose parents work in the kitchen going to school with kids whose parents work upstairs, by choice and practicality rather than by force.

The program will be staggeringly expensive and hard to get past the state legislatures.

Expensive, yes—just like Social Security—and difficult to pass—just like health care reform. Now is likely not a propitious time to be discussing such a massive reform; however, I believe it is the only way to really do what so many are claiming to want to do, and to do it fairly. There will be intense opposition to the plan. It is one thing for a state legislature to enact a modest voucher program whose funds are deducted from money that the state would have been spending to educate poor children anyway. It is quite another to call for a plan that requires additional money and lots of it.

There will be opposition by teachers' unions and administrators.

I am not as certain that individual teachers, as opposed to the unions, would be as worried as policymakers might expect, and the reason is this:

Because there has been no cross-class coalition in education, teachers' unions have borne much of the burden for fighting to ensure equitable funding and resisting any attempts at eroding the public commitment to educating all children. This includes paying teachers enough to attract and retain competent individuals. If a system of education were irrevocably equitable and sufficiently funded, then individual teachers might not be as strongly opposed as their union leadership, particularly since middle-class parents would fight very hard against a system that tried to get by on slim funding.

There will be waste and corruption associated with the redistribution of many billions of dollars within individual states.

Yes, there will be. Any innovation will be accompanied by waste, mismanagement, crazy schemes, and foolish ideas (just look at the development of the internet). However, we seem to tolerate, as a society, much more of this kind of thing with private-sector innovations rather than public-sector innovations.

Transportation will present challenges, particularly in rural areas.

This is a serious issue, but transportation issues are going to arise with any reform plan that hopes to remedy the serious problems of economic segregation in American education.

There will be a "race to the bottom" as states try to set scholarship amounts low to keep taxes down.

I doubt this will happen. Powerful business interests in individual school districts do sometimes use this power to keep spending and taxes down. However, if parents were united across a state, and not fragmented, then those interests lined up against spending on education would be fighting against a much more powerful adversary. Also, enlightened business leaders and state officials would likely recognize that investment in education is crucial to a state's economic future. It might just become more attractive for a state to lure businesses with an outstanding public school system rather than play the game of selective tax breaks for companies that might go looking for greener pastures.

My political advice to those who are worried by choice is this: Stop fighting it. Parents demand it. It has beneficial bureaucratic consequences, and we have to do something. But make school choice live up to its promises, and don't settle for choice on the cheap. Push instead for a system that maximizes parental choice and school autonomy but is designed in such a way to ensure universal, equitable funding created and sustained by a coalition of parents in all classes fighting for the same program. Clarence Stone and colleagues point to a lamentable state in American education that they call "fiscal federalism," in which those parents with more resources gravitate to advantaged school districts, spending their money and politics in their narrow spheres.[24] I would argue for something approaching fiscal nationalism, in which all parents are bound together in securing resources for education, as is currently the case with universal programs such as Social Security.[25]

The results presented in this book have established that market-based reforms can change the behaviors of parents and public school principals, both beneficially and destructively, depending on the institutional and social contexts of those reforms and the levels of political voice in the community. School choice has the potential to make education in the United States better or the potential to provide another strain on an already strained system. The question is how we go about it. We may be talking about bureaucratic reinvention and democratic reinvigoration, or we may be talking about hastened obsolescence and increasing inequality. Neither outcome is predetermined.

Appendix A | Supplementary Tables for Chapter 2

TABLE A.1. Attrition in the Milwaukee Voucher Data

	Interviewed in Following Spring (1)	Not Interviewed (2)
Parent accepted into choice program	0.72	0.61
	[0.68–0.77]	[0.57–0.66]
Fall reports on previous year's participation		
Belong to PTA	0.21	0.23
	[0.17–0.25]	[0.18–0.27]
Attend PTA meetings	0.53	0.57
	[0.48–0.58]	[0.52–0.62]
Actively participate in PTA	0.47	0.51
	[0.42–0.52]	[0.46–0.56]
PTA summary measure	1.21	1.31
	[1.11–1.32]	[1.20–1.42]
Demographic characteristics		
Household income	4.32	4.67
	[4.13–4.51]	[4.47–4.88]
Parental education	4.22	4.21
	[4.09–4.36]	[4.08–4.34]
N	387	389

Source: Data from Witte and Thorn 1995.
Note: Confidence intervals (95%) in brackets.

TABLE A.2.   Choice Accepted and Choice Rejected in the Milwaukee Voucher
Data

	Choice Accepted (1)	Choice Rejected (2)
Fall reports on previous year's participation		
Belong to PTA	0.23	0.16
	[0.18–0.28]	[0.09–0.23]
Attend PTA meetings	0.52	0.56
	[0.46–0.58]	[0.47–0.66]
Actively participate in PTA	0.47	0.47
	[0.41–0.53]	[0.38–0.57]
PTA summary measure	1.22	1.19
	[1.09–1.35]	[1.00–1.39]
Demographic characteristics		
Household income	4.30	4.40
	[4.06–4.52]	[4.03–4.76]
Parental education	4.19	4.30
	[4.03–4.35]	[4.05–4.55]
N	279	108

Source: Data from Witte and Thorn 1995.
Note: Confidence intervals (95%) in brackets.

TABLE A.3.   Means and Standard Deviations of Variables in Table 2.1

	Mean (1)	Standard Deviation (2)
Parent applied for choice program	0.12	(0.33)
PTA involvement		
Belong to PTA	0.21	(0.41)
Attend PTA meetings	0.38	(0.49)
Actively participate in PTA	0.37	(0.48)
PTA summary measure	0.97	(1.07)
Demographic characteristics		
Student is member of a minority group	0.62	(0.48)
Language other than English	0.02	(0.15)
Household income	5.77	(2.70)
Parental education	4.05	(1.50)
School to parent contact about fund-raising and volunteering (0–3)	0.58	(0.77)

Source: Data from Witte and Thorn 1995.

TABLE A.4.   Means and Standard Deviations of Variables in Table 2.3

	Mean (1)	Standard Deviation (2)
Parent accepted into choice program	0.72	(0.45)
One-year change in PTA activities		
Belong to PTA	0.22	(0.55)
Attend PTA meetings	0.09	(0.64)
Actively participate in PTA	0.14	(0.62)
PTA summary measure	0.44	(1.21)
Demographic characteristics		
Household income	4.26	(1.96)
Parental education	4.21	(1.35)
Change in school to parent contact about fund-raising and volunteering	0.29	(1.07)

Source: Data from Witte and Thorn 1995.

TABLE A.5.   Means and Standard Deviations of Variables in 1996 National Household Education Survey

	Mean (1)	Standard Deviation (2)
Child in public choice setting	0.13	(0.34)
Child in private school	0.11	(0.31)
Age of parent (primary caregiver)	41.16	(7.42)
Parent is female	0.78	(0.41)
Language other than English spoken at home	0.09	(0.28)
Household income	7.59	(2.95)
Highest degree earned (parent/caregiver)	3.06	(1.20)
Student is member of a minority group	0.33	(0.47)
Student's grade level	8.81	(1.98)
School participation	0.92	(0.72)
Political participation	1.51	(1.25)
N	9,230	

Source: 1996 National Household Education Survey.

TABLE A.6.   The Decision to Exit in the 1996 National Household Education Survey

	Public Choice (1)	Private School (2)
Age of parent (primary caregiver)	−0.005*	0.016***
	(0.002)	(0.003)
Parent is female	0.06	0.12**
	(0.05)	(0.05)
Language other than	−0.09	0.03
English spoken at home	(0.07)	(0.09)
Household income	−0.04***	0.03***
	(0.01)	(0.01)
Highest degree earned (parent/caregiver)	0.08***	0.15***
	(0.02)	(0.02)
Student is member of a minority group	0.31***	0.001
	(0.04)	(0.051)
Student's grade level	0.06***	0.02**
	(0.03)	(0.01)
School participation	0.06**	0.52***
	(0.03)	(0.03)
Political participation	0.08***	0.01
	(0.02)	(0.02)
Constant	−1.67***	−3.46***
	(0.13)	(0.16)
N	8,234	8,040
LR chi^2 (14)	198.33	689.09
Prob > chi^2	0.00	0.00

Source: 1996 National Household Education Survey. Columns 1 and 2 present probit regression results.
  Note: The dependent variable is a parent's decision to enroll the child in a public choice school, column 1, or a private school, column 2. Standard error estimates are in parentheses.
  *p < .1;   **p < .05;   ***p < .01, two-tailed.

Appendix B | Supplementary Tables for Chapter 4

TABLE B.1.   Means and Standard Deviations in Minnesota Schools Survey

	Mean (1)	Standard Deviation (2)
Charter school in district	0.28	(0.45)
School is charter school	0.04	(0.19)
School characteristics		
Number of students (100s)	5.59	(4.17)
Highest grade offered	8.84	(3.08)
Ungraded school	0.02	(0.10)
Hispanic (%)	0.02	(0.08)
African American (%)	0.06	(0.12)
Free lunch eligible (%)	0.22	(0.18)
Limited English proficient (%)	0.05	(0.11)
Principal characteristics		
10 or more years of experience as a principal	0.45	(0.50)
10 or more years of experience as a teacher	0.67	(0.47)
Ph.D.	0.13	(0.34)
Time spent on activities		
Facilitating achievement of the school's mission	3.02	(1.12)
Supervising faculty	3.08	(0.93)
Guiding development of the curriculum	2.76	(1.00)
Building relationships with the parent community	3.19	(0.90)
Maintaining the physical security of students and staff	3.18	(1.02)
Managing facilities	3.03	(1.02)
Completing administrative tasks	3.91	(0.90)
Mean score	3.17	(0.51)
Influence		
Parents	3.17	(0.96)
Principal	3.86	(0.91)
Teachers	3.77	(0.92)
State and local administration	3.93	(0.68)
Relative influence of parents and principals	0.69	(1.00)
Effects of parental involvement on principals' influence		
Setting performance standards	3.49	(0.71)

(continued)

TABLE B.1—*Continued*

	Mean (1)	Standard Deviation (2)
Establishing curriculum	3.42	(0.68)
Hiring teachers	3.11	(0.63)
Evaluating teachers	3.05	(0.64)
Setting discipline policy	3.55	(0.76)
Deciding how the budget is spent	3.18	(0.71)
Whether or not parents are offered the chance to participate		
Parents as volunteers	0.95	(0.22)
Parents involved in school governance	0.86	(0.35)
Parents involved in budget decisions	0.79	(0.41)
Parents participating		
In open house or back to school night	3.64	(0.73)
Regularly scheduled parent-teacher conferences	3.80	(0.54)
As volunteers	2.06	(0.95)
In school governance	1.35	(0.61)
In budget decisions	1.22	(0.51)
Trend in parental participation	3.36	(0.85)

Source: Minnesota Schools Survey 2003. Student demographic data from the Minnesota Department of Education 2003.

TABLE B.2.   The Effects of Parental Involvement on Principals' Influence (full results)

	Setting Performance Standards (1)	Hiring Teachers (2)	Evaluating Teachers (3)	Budget (4)
Charter school in district	0.13	0.28***	0.19*	0.26***
	(0.09)	(0.10)	(0.10)	(0.10)
School is charter school	0.86***	0.99***	0.54**	0.53**
	(0.21)	(0.21)	(0.22)	(0.21)
Number of students (100s)	0.01	0.004	0.01	0.12
	(0.01)	(0.011)	(0.01)	(0.11)
Highest grade offered	−0.02	−0.05***	−0.01	−0.05***
	(0.01)	(0.01)	(0.01)	(0.01)
Ungraded school	0.36	0.01	0.18	0.37
	(0.35)	(0.38)	(0.38)	(0.36)
Hispanic (%)	−0.78	−1.54**	−0.59	−0.91
	(0.73)	(0.77)	(0.78)	(0.74)
African American (%)	0.28	0.18	0.43	0.99**
	(0.44)	(0.48)	(0.48)	(0.45)
Free lunch eligible (%)	−1.18***	−0.62*	−0.51	−0.34
	(0.32)	(0.36)	(0.36)	(0.34)
Limited English proficient (%)	0.79	1.12*	−0.00	1.83***
	(0.63)	(0.68)	(0.83)	(0.64)
At least 10 years principal experience	0.03	−0.04	−0.01	0.04
	(0.08)	(0.08)	(0.08)	(0.08)
At least 10 years teaching experience	−0.01	0.11	0.07	0.21***
	(0.01)	(0.09)	(0.09)	(0.08)
Ph.D.	0.24**	0.32**	0.11	0.06
	(0.12)	(0.13)	(0.13)	(0.12)
Cut points	−2.63	−2.28	−1.71	−1.99
	−1.83	−1.94	−1.43	−1.44
	−0.28	0.54	0.96	0.58
	1.47	1.87	2.52	2.11
N	928	928	928	928
LR chi^2 (14)	46.16	63.05	19.62	94.25
Prob > chi^2	0.00	0.00	0.07	0.00

Source: Minnesota Schools Survey 2003. Student demographic data from the Minnesota Department of Education 2003.

Note: Columns 1 through 4 present coefficient estimates from separate ordered probit regression results. Standard error estimates are in parentheses.

*p < 0.1;   **p < .05;   ***p < .01, two-tailed.

TABLE B.3. Charter Schools and the Use of Principals' Time (full results)

	Achieve Mission (1)	Supervise Faculty (2)	Develop Curriculum (3)	Parents (4)	Security (5)	Mean (6)
Charter school in district	0.33***	0.07	-0.07	0.07	-0.10	0.06
	(0.09)	(0.09)	(0.09)	(0.09)	(0.09)	(0.04)
School is charter school	0.68***	-0.27	0.15	0.48**	-0.49**	0.05
	(0.21)	(0.20)	(0.20)	(0.20)	(0.21)	(0.10)
Number of students (100s)	0.02*	0.01	0.001	-0.01	0.02**	0.01
	(0.01)	(0.01)	(0.010)	(0.01)	(0.01)	(0.01)
Highest grade offered	-0.05***	-0.01	-0.01	-0.07***	0.03***	-0.02**
	(0.01)	(0.01)	(0.01)	(0.01)	(0.01)	(0.01)
Ungraded school	0.16	0.64*	0.12	0.37	-0.32	0.20
	(0.34)	(0.35)	(0.34)	(0.35)	(0.34)	(0.16)
Hispanic (%)	0.67	-0.05	0.24	0.17	2.28***	0.57*
	(0.70)	(0.68)	(0.76)	(0.68)	(0.68)	(0.32)
African American (%)	0.41	1.00**	0.61	1.38***	0.74*	0.43**
	(0.44)	(0.43)	(0.43)	(0.43)	(0.43)	(0.21)
Free lunch eligible (%)	-0.04	-0.22	0.13	-1.67***	-0.09	-0.14
	(0.31)	(0.31)	(0.31)	(0.32)	(0.31)	(0.15)
Limited English proficient (%)	0.95	0.71	0.73	0.73	-0.98	0.15
	(0.60)	(0.60)	(0.60)	(0.60)	(0.59)	(0.28)
At least 10 years principal experience	0.05	-0.01	-0.07	-0.07	0.06	-0.01
	(0.07)	(0.07)	(0.07)	(0.07)	(0.07)	(0.03)
At least 10 years teaching experience	0.11	0.03	0.16**	0.21***	0.15**	0.08**
	(0.08)	(0.07)	(0.08)	(0.08)	(0.08)	(0.04)
Ph.D.	0.24**	0.05	0.14	0.01	-0.07	-0.01
	(0.11)	(0.11)	(0.11)	(0.11)	(0.11)	(0.05)

Cut points	-1.56	-1.98	-1.41	-2.93	-1.20	3.16***
						(0.08)
	-0.39	-0.58	-0.13	-1.43	-0.11	
	0.58	0.61	0.82	-0.38	0.94	
	1.23	1.50	1.68	0.58	1.82	
N	910	910	910	910	910	910
LR chi² (14)	107.82	38.78	34.11	85.26	38.20	—
Prob > chi²	0.00	0.00	0.00	0.00	0.00	$R^2 = 0.06$

Source: Minnesota Schools Survey 2003. Student demographic data from the Minnesota Department of Education 2003.

Note: Columns 1 through 5 present coefficient estimates from separate ordered probit regression results. Column 6 presents coefficient estimates from OLS regression. Standard error estimates are in parentheses.

*$p < 0.1$;   **$p < .05$;   ***$p < .01$, two-tailed.

TABLE B.4.   Offering Parents the Opportunity to Participate (full results)

	As Volunteers (1)	In School Governance (2)	In Budget Decisions (3)
Charter school in district	0.02	0.25*	0.11
	(0.24)	(0.15)	(0.13)
School is charter school	0.12	1.34**	1.00***
	(0.38)	(0.52)	(0.37)
Number of students (100s)	0.05*	0.05***	0.03*
	(0.02)	(0.02)	(0.02)
Highest grade offered	−0.19***	−0.04**	−0.03*
	(0.03)	(0.02)	(0.02)
Ungraded school	−0.25	0.15	0.37
	(0.46)	(0.45)	(0.45)
Hispanic (%)	−0.66	−2.19	−2.95**
	(2.01)	(1.44)	(1.28)
African American (%)	−0.03	−0.26	−0.46
	(1.19)	(0.81)	(0.67)
Free lunch eligible (%)	−0.39	−0.09	−0.004
	(0.66)	(0.48)	(0.42)
Limited English proficient (%)	1.24	3.42**	4.46***
	(1.70)	(1.46)	(1.29)
At least 10 years principal experience	−0.30*	−0.07	0.002
	(0.17)	(0.11)	(0.010)
At least 10 years teaching experience	−0.03	0.20*	0.14
	(0.17)	(0.11)	(0.10)
Ph.D.	0.20	0.15	0.15
	(0.30)	(0.19)	(0.16)
Constant	3.57***	0.91***	0.70***
	(0.42)	(0.24)	(0.21)
N	930	930	930
LR chi^2 (14)	64.30	53.90	48.54
Prob > chi^2	0.00	0.00	0.00

Source: Minnesota Schools Survey 2003. Student demographic data from the Minnesota Department of Education 2003.

Note: Columns (1) through (3) present coefficient estimates from probit regression results. Standard error estimates are in parentheses.

*$p < 0.1$;   **$p < .05$;   ***$p < .01$, two-tailed.

TABLE B.5.   The Level of Parental Participation (full results)

	As Volunteers (1)	Governance (2)	Budget (3)	Trend (4)
Charter school in district	0.04	–0.16	0.07	–0.08
	(0.10)	(0.12)	(0.13)	(0.09)
School is charter school	0.34	0.61***	0.68***	0.56***
	(0.23)	(0.23)	(0.25)	(0.21)
Number of students (100s)	0.002	–0.01	–0.02	0.03***
	(0.010)	(0.01)	(0.02)	(0.01)
Highest grade offered	–0.18***	–0.03*	–0.02	–0.05***
	(0.01)	(0.02)	(0.02)	(0.01)
Ungraded school	–0.28	0.53	0.13	–0.24
	(0.42)	(0.40)	(0.49)	(0.33)
Hispanic (%)	0.81	0.68	1.75*	–0.94
	(0.80)	(0.90)	(1.00)	(0.78)
African American (%)	0.79	–0.22	–0.38	0.00
	(0.49)	(0.57)	(0.73)	(0.44)
Free lunch eligible (%)	–3.05***	–0.71*	–0.89*	0.73**
	(0.36)	(0.40)	(0.48)	(0.31)
Limited English proficient (%)	0.18	0.50	0.51	–0.25
	(0.68)	(0.78)	(0.90)	(0.61)
At least 10 years principal experience	0.11	0.14	0.27**	–0.05
	(0.08)	(0.10)	(0.11)	(0.07)
At least 10 years teaching experience	0.10	0.11	0.40***	0.03
	(0.08)	(0.10)	(0.12)	(0.08)
Ph.D.	0.29**	0.12	0.11	0.18
	(0.12)	(0.14)	(0.15)	(0.11)
Cut points	–2.54	0.29	0.96	–2.09
	–1.11	1.50	2.09	–1.31
	–0.42	1.94	2.57	0.00
				1.40
N	885	796	732	923
LR chi^2 (14)	297.50	24.05	36.14	39.51
Prob > chi^2	0.00	0.02	0.00	0.00

Source: Minnesota Schools Survey 2003. Student demographic data from the Minnesota Department of Education 2003.

Note: Columns (1) through (4) present coefficient estimates from probit regression results. Standard error estimates are in parentheses.

*p < 0.1;   **p < .05;   ***p < .01, two-tailed.

Appendix C | Supplementary Tables and Material for Chapter 5

TABLE C.1.   Means and Standard Deviations of Variables in New Jersey April Budget Election Study

	Mean (1)	Standard Deviation (2)
Charter school host district	0.29	(0.45)
Turnout	10.97	(4.90)
Budget success	0.73	(0.44)
Current year special question	0.10	(0.30)
Previous year special question	0.09	(0.28)
Special questions in both years	0.03	(0.18)
Black (%)	17.08	(20.96)
Asian (%)	5.42	(6.62)
Hispanic (%)	14.65	(14.18)
College graduates (%)	31.30	(16.22)
Senior citizens (%)	13.47	(4.76)
Property tax rate	2.58	(0.71)
Property tax base (1,000s)	95.32	(115.14)
State aid in budget (%)	32.76	(28.09)

Source: New Jersey April Budget Election Study 2003.

Matching Procedures for New Jersey April Budget Election Data

I employed a satisficing procedure to match the districts according to a vector of nine demographic and school finance characteristics, moving away from the host district—both geographically and in my target ranges of the key variables—until I found a match that fulfilled my criteria. The point of departure was to restrict my search for noncharter matching districts within the same district factor group as the host district. The DFG is an indicator of the socioeconomic status bases on U.S. Census data, assigned to all but the smallest school districts by the New Jersey Department of Education. It consists of a letter code ranging from A for the poorest districts, to J for the wealthiest, with combined categories for CD, DE, FG, and GH. It is assembled from demographic data on the high school completion rate, college attendance rate, occupational status of adult household members, population density, unemployment rate, and the percentages of district residents in poverty.

Using the DFG ranking as a starting point eliminated two charter school host districts from my initial list of twenty-two—Allenhurst and Interlaken—as they are not assigned a district factor group by the Department of Education. In one case, that of Plainfield, I was forced to move from a DFG rating of A to B because of a failure to find any districts that came sufficiently close to my other search criteria. In all but one case (that of Hoboken), I was able to pair Abbott districts with each other, so named because of their status as targeted districts under New Jersey's school finance litigation.

Having restricted the initial search to districts with similar DFG ratings, I then attempted to find the best matches possible on a vector of nine district and school finance characteristics: the average tax base of the district, the average percentage of state aid for that district, the average property tax rate, the district's population, and the percentage of residents who were African American, Hispanic, Asian, and college educated. I obtained average values by calculating the mean values for that district in 1996 and 2002, to capture any trends that might have taken place during the seven years covered by my study. It quickly became apparent that, if I tried to match on the percentages of African American and Hispanic residents separately, I would not find any successful matches for a large percentage of my charter school districts; therefore I concentrated on matching according to the combined percentages of these two racial and ethnic groups.

I was also forced to drop two more charter school districts from my study. Atlantic City, although defined as an A district, had an average per-resident property tax base of more than $185,000, a figure more in line with FG and GH districts. I assume that this is due to the presence of casinos, hotels, and other valuable commercial property in the district. In addition—after the analyses were completed—I did not include Ocean City, a very small district in Cape May County and its matched pair in the study. Ocean City had a voter turnout in excess of 30 percent in some elections and—since it is a charter school host district—was likely to bias my results in favor of finding positive effects on turnout from the presence of charter schools. Finally, and most important, I made no changes to the districts that I had chosen as matched pairs once the empirical analysis had begun. Other researchers may find better and closer matches; however, it would have been irresponsible and suspect to try to find "better" matches once I had seen the initial results.

TABLE C.2. Matching School District Characteristics from New Jersey April Budget Election Study

District	County (1)	District Factor Group (2)	Average Tax Base (1,000s) (3)	Average State Aid (%) (4)	Average Tax Rate (mills) (5)	1990 Population (6)	Black (%) (7)	Hispanic (%) (8)	Asian (%) (9)
Pleasantville	Atlantic	A	30.0	76.6	3.13	16,027	57.7	21.9	2.0
Bridgeton	Cumberland	A	18.6	89.9	2.72	18,942	41.8	24.5	0.7
Camden City	Camden	A	11.7	94.7	3.81	87,492	53.3	38.8	2.5
Irvington Township	Essex	A	21.7	80.1	4.67	61,018	81.7	8.4	1.1
Asbury Park	Monmouth	A	25.6	83.7	3.63	16,799	62.1	15.6	0.7
Perth Amboy	Middlesex	A	35.0	77.7	2.72	41,967	10.0	69.8	1.5
Hoboken	Hudson	B	79.7	28.1	2.33	33,397	4.3	20.2	4.3
Kearny	Hudson	B	49.5	33.3	3.16	34,874	4.0	27.3	5.5
Bradley Beach	Monmouth	B	79.4	17.6	2.60	4,475	3.9	12.8	1.5
Stafford Township	Ocean	B	93.0	30.3	2.04	13,325	0.7	2.4	1.0
Plainfield	Union	B	33.4	76.3	3.16	46,567	61.2	25.2	0.9
Elizabeth	Union	A	32.0	77.9	2.73	110,002	20.0	50.0	2.3
South Blemar	Monmouth	CD	74.8	16.1	2.28	1,482	7.8	10.1	1.3
Highlands Borough	Monmouth	CD	61.7	17.0	3.13	4,849	1.6	4.1	1.0
Belmar	Monmouth	DE	91.7	15.5	2.23	5,877	3.5	6.8	1.0
Point Pleasant Beach	Ocean	DE	168.5	8.3	1.71	5,112	0.5	4.4	1.0
Ocean City	Cape May	DE	304.6	9.6	1.40	15,512	4.3	2.0	0.6
Cape May City	Cape May	DE	257.0	13.4	1.24	4,668	5.3	3.8	0.4
Clifton	Passaic	DE	72.8	14.4	2.45	71,742	2.9	19.8	6.4
Bloomfield Township	Essex	DE	52.6	19.2	3.22	45,061	11.7	14.5	8.4

(continued)

TABLE C.2—Continued

District	County (1)	District Factor Group (2)	Average Tax Base (1,000s) (3)	Average State Aid (%) (4)	Average Tax Rate (mills) (5)	1990 Population (6)	Black (%) (7)	Hispanic (%) (8)	Asian (%) (9)
Hamilton Township	Mercer	FG	55.4	38.6	2.52	86,553	8.2	5.1	2.6
Old Bridge Township	Middlesex	FG	57.1	35.5	2.55	56,475	5.3	7.6	10.8
Edison Township	Middlesex	FG	85.3	9.6	2.12	88,680	6.9	6.4	29.3
Piscataway Township	Middlesex	FG	68.8	19.1	2.38	47,089	20.3	7.9	24.8
Teaneck	Bergen	GH	79.0	8.0	2.91	37,825	28.8	10.5	7.1
Westwood Regional	Bergen	GH	163.8	7.5	2.01	19,692	3.4	4.7	5.0
Highland Park	Middlesex	GH	54.8	19.1	3.04	13,279	7.9	8.2	13.6
East Windsor Regional	Mercer	GH	54.8	28.8	2.98	27,479	8.8	15.5	8.4
Avon Borough	Monmouth	GH	157.3	8.3	1.67	2,165	0.5	2.4	0.9
Oceanport Borough	Monmouth	GH	100.3	8.1	2.12	6,146	2.0	2.1	0.8
Deal Borough	Monmouth	GH	695.6	8.4	0.88	1,179	1.2	5.0	0.3
Sea Bright	Monmouth	GH	304.6	14.5	1.98	1,693	0.1	1.4	0.3
Franklin Township	Somerset	GH	87.3	24.2	2.14	42,780	26.0	8.1	12.7
North Brunswick Township	Middlesex	GH	71.3	17.5	2.43	31,287	15.3	10.4	14.2
Princeton Regional	Mercer	I	135.8	7.0	1.93	25,214	5.9	6.2	8.8
Lawrence Township	Mercer	I	94.9	9.7	2.31	25,787	9.3	4.6	7.9

Source: New Jersey April Budget Election Study 2003. District demographic data from New Jersey Legislative District Data Book (years 1996–2003).
Note: Charter school districts are represented in first district of each matched pair shown.

Notes

CHAPTER 1

1. "New Jersey's New Governor: Excerpts from Whitman's Address on Leadership, Taxes, and Schools," *New York Times,* January 19, 1994.

2. Mary McGrath, "Coalition Backs School Voucher Proposal," *(Bergen) Record,* October 12, 1994.

3. Milton Friedman, "The Role of Government in Education," in Robert A. Solo, ed., *Economics and the Public Interest* (New Brunswick, NJ: Rutgers University Press, 1955).

4. John E. Chubb and Terry M. Moe, *Politics, Markets, and America's Schools* (Washington, DC: Brookings Institution Press, 1990).

5. Thomas T. Holyoke and Jeffrey R. Henig, "All for One or Each for Its Own? Charter Schools and Collective Action in the District of Columbia" (paper presented at the annual meeting of the Midwest Political Science Association, Chicago, April 19–22, 2001).

6. Martin Rein, "The Social Structure of Institutions: Neither Public nor Private," in Sheila B. Kamerman and Alfred J. Kahn, eds., *Privatization and the Welfare State* (Princeton: Princeton University Press, 1989).

7. Robert A. Dahl, *A Preface to Economic Democracy* (Berkeley: University of California Press, 1985), 7.

8. Jane J. Mansbridge, "The Rise and Fall of Self-Interest in the Explanation of Political Life," in Jane J. Mansbridge, ed., *Beyond Self-Interest* (Chicago: University of Chicago Press, 1990).

9. Jennifer L. Hochschild and Nathan Scovronick, *The American Dream and the Public Schools* (New York: Oxford University Press, 2003).

10. Jeffrey Henig, *Rethinking School Choice: Limits of the Market Metaphor* (Princeton: Princeton University Press, 1994), 20; R. Kenneth Godwin and Frank R. Kemerer, *School Choice Tradeoffs: Liberty, Equity, and Diversity* (Austin: University of Texas Press, 2002). Godwin and Kemerer apply the trade-off between equality and liberty to the case of school choice, arguing that choice policies can endanger the transmission of societal values by privileging parental rights in the moral education of their children.

11. Albert O. Hirschman, *Exit, Voice, and Loyalty: Responses to Decline in Firms, Organizations, and States* (Cambridge, MA: Harvard University Press, 1970), 4–5.

12. Mancur Olson, *The Logic of Collective Action: Public Goods and the Theory of Groups* (Cambridge, MA: Harvard University Press, 1971).

13. Paul E. Teske et al., "Establishing the Micro Foundations of a Macro Theory: Information Movers and the Competitive Local Market for Public Goods," *American Political Science Review* 87, no. 3 (1993); Mark Schneider et al., "Shopping for Schools: In the Land of the Blind, the One-Eyed Parent May Be Enough," *American Journal of Political Science* 42, no. 3 (1998).

14. Hirschman, *Exit, Voice, and Loyalty,* 51.

15. See John Gaventa, *Power and Powerlessness: Quiescence and Rebellion in an Appalachian Valley* (Urbana: University of Illinois Press, 1980).

16. Hirschman, *Exit, Voice, and Loyalty,* 105.

17. Mark Schneider, Paul Teske, and Melissa Marschall, *Choosing Schools: Consumer Choice and the Quality of American Education* (Princeton: Princeton University Press, 2000), 12.

18. Ibid., 269.

19. Ibid.

20. Clarence N. Stone et al., *Building Civic Capacity: The Politics of Reforming Urban Schools* (Lawrence: University Press of Kansas, 2001).

21. Ibid., 70.

22. Ibid., 1.

23. John F. Witte, *The Market Approach to Education: An Analysis of America's First Voucher Program* (Princeton: Princeton University Press, 2000); idem, "The Milwaukee Voucher Experiment," *Educational Evaluation and Policy Management* 20 (1998); Cecilia Elena Rouse, "Schools and Student Achievement: More Evidence from the Milwaukee Parental Choice Program," *Federal Reserve Bank of New York Economic Policy Review* (1998).

24. William G. Howell and Paul E. Peterson (with Patrick J. Wolf and David E. Campbell), *The Education Gap: Vouchers and Urban Schools* (Washington, DC: Brookings Institution Press, 2002).

25. United States General Accounting Office, "School Vouchers: Publicly Funded Programs in Cleveland and Milwaukee," *Report to the Honorable Judd Gregg, U.S. Senate* (Washington, DC, 2001).

26. William T. Garner and Jane Hannaway, "Private Schools: The Client Connection," in Michael E. Manley-Casimir, ed., *Family Choice in Schooling* (Lexington, MA: Lexington Books, 1982). The term *client connection* is theirs.

27. Jeffrey L. Pressman and Aaron Wildavsky, *Implementation: How Great Expectations in Washington Are Dashed in Oakland* (Berkeley: University of California Press, 1984); Daniel P. Moynihan, *Maximum Feasible Misunderstanding: Community Action in the War on Poverty* (New York: Free Press, 1969).

28. Frederick M. Hess, "Hints of the Pick-Axe: Competition and Public Schooling in Milwaukee," in Paul E. Peterson and David E. Campbell, eds., *Charters, Vouchers, and Public Education* (Washington, DC: Brookings Institution Press, 2001).

29. These relationships are usually referred to as *principal-agent relationships.* The problem with the terminology, in my case, is that school principals are the agents, and citizens and customers are the principals, which is a bit confusing, though it lends itself to the sort of bad pun that political scientists are often guilty

of. See Terry M. Moe, "The New Economics of Organization," *American Journal of Political Science* 28, no. 4 (1984); Jonathan Bendor and Terry M. Moe, "An Adaptive Model of Bureaucratic Politics," *American Political Science Review* 79, no. 3 (1985); Stephen A. Ross, "The Economic Theory of Agency: The Principal's Problem," *American Economic Review* 63, no. 2 (1973).

30. Avinash Dixit, Gene M. Grossman, and Elhanan Helpman, "Common Agency and Coordination: General Theory and Application to Government Policy Making," *Journal of Political Economy* 105, no. 4 (1997); B. Douglas Bernheim and Michael D. Whinston, "Common Agency," *Econometrica* 54, no. 4 (1986).

31. This discussion of an agency web is based on a description of the educator's role in influencing the outcomes of desegregation policy described by Mark Chesler, Bunyan I. Bryant, and James Crowfoot, *Making Desegregation Work: A Professional's Guide to Effecting Change* (Beverly Hills, CA: Sage Publications, 1981). See also Jennifer L. Hochschild, *The New American Dilemma: Liberal Democracy and School Desegregation* (New Haven: Yale University Press, 1984), 149–53.

32. Avinash Dixit, "Power of Incentives in Private versus Public Organizations," *American Economic Review* 87, no. 2 (1997).

33. Sidney Verba, Kay Lehman Schlozman, and Henry E. Brady, *Voice and Equality: Civic Volunteerism in American Politics* (Cambridge, MA: Harvard University Press, 1995); Henry E. Brady, Sidney Verba, and Key Lehman Schlozman, "Beyond SES: A Resource Model of Political Participation," *American Political Science Review* 89, no. 2 (1995).

34. Paul Pierson, "When Effect Becomes Cause: Policy Feedback and Political Change," *World Politics* 45 (1993). Pierson developed the theoretical concerns and defined much of the agenda for current policy-feedback research, though, as Pierson notes, the central idea goes back to E. E. Schattschneider's (1935) observation that "new policies create a new politics" (288).

35. Anne Schneider and Helen Ingram, "Social Construction of Target Populations: Implications for Politics and Policy," *American Political Science Review* 87, no. 2 (1993); Joe Soss, "Lessons of Welfare: Policy Design, Political Learning, and Political Action," *American Political Science Review* 93, no. 2 (1999); Pierson, "When Effect Becomes Cause."

36. Suzanne Mettler, "Bringing the State Back in to Civic Engagement: Policy Feedback Effects of the G.I. Bill for World War II Veterans," *American Political Science Review* 96, no. 2 (2002); idem, *Civic Generation: The G.I. Bill in Veterans' Lives* (New York: Oxford University Press, forthcoming).

37. Andrea Louise Campbell, "Self-Interest, Social Security, and the Distinctive Participation Patterns of Seniors," *American Political Science Review* 96, no. 3 (2002); idem, *How Policies Make Citizens* (Princeton: Princeton University Press, 2003).

38. Theda Skocpol, *Protecting Soldiers and Mothers: The Political Origins of Social Policy in the United States* (Cambridge, MA: Harvard University Press, 1992); Stephen Skowronek, *Building a New American State: The Expansion of National Administrative Capacities, 1877–1920* (New York: Cambridge University Press, 1982).

39. Theda Skocpol, *Diminished Democracy: From Membership to Management in American Civic Life* (Norman: University of Oklahoma Press, 2003).

40. The distinction between bridging and bonding is from Robert Putnam, *Bowling Alone: The Collapse and Revival of American Community* (New York: Simon and Schuster, 2000).

41. Skocpol, *Diminished Democracy,* 264.

42. Campbell, *How Policies Make Citizens,* 2.

43. Pierson, "When Effect Becomes Cause"; Suzanne Mettler and Joe Soss, "The Consequences of Public Policy for Democratic Citizenship: Bridging Policy Studies and Mass Politics," *Perspectives on Politics* 2, no. 1 (2004). Mettler and Soss argue that researchers and policymakers need to return to consideration of "the ways that policies, once created, affect the strength and logic of self-governance" (56).

44. Jacob Hacker et al., "Inequality and Public Policy," Task Force Report on Inequality and American Democracy, American Political Science Association (2004).

45. I am indebted to an anonymous reviewer for clarification of this point.

46. I thank anonymous reviewers, charitable and critical, for pointing this out.

47. Dahl, *A Preface to Economic Democracy,* 4.

CHAPTER 2

1. Hirschman, *Exit, Voice, and Loyalty,* 45–46.

2. *Griffin v. County School Board of Prince Edward County,* 377 U.S. 218 (1964).

3. United States General Accounting Office, "School Vouchers."

4. This may change, however, as entire states are contemplating or enacting voucher programs. Participation, however, will likely remain voluntary in suburban schools.

5. United States General Accounting Office, "School Vouchers"; idem, "Insufficient Research to Determine Effectiveness of Selected Private Education Companies," *Report to the Ranking Minority Member, Subcommittee on the District of Columbia, Committee on Appropriations, House of Representatives* (Washington, DC, 2002).

6. Howell and Peterson, *The Education Gap;* William G. Howell, Patrick J. Wolf, Paul E. Peterson, and David E. Campbell, "Effects of School Choice on Test Scores," in Paul E. Peterson and David E. Campbell, eds., *Charters, Vouchers, and Public Education* (Washington, DC: Brookings Institution Press, 2001).

7. Alan B. Krueger and Pei Zhu, "Another Look at the New York City School Voucher Experiment," *American Behavioral Scientist* 47, no. 5 (2004); idem, "Inefficiency, Subsample Selection Bias, and Nonrobustness: A Response to Paul E. Peterson and William G. Howell," *American Behavioral Scientist* 47, no. 5 (2004); Paul E. Peterson and William G. Howell, "Efficiency, Bias, and Classification Schemes: A Response to Alan B. Krueger and Pei Zhu," *American Behavioral Scientist* 47, no. 5 (2004).

8. Henry Levin, "Educational Vouchers: Effectiveness, Choice, and Costs," *Journal of Policy Analysis and Management* 17, no. 3 (1998); Martin Carnoy,

"School Improvement: Is Privatization the Answer?" in Jane Hannaway and Martin Carnoy, eds., *Decentralization and School Improvement* (San Francisco: Jossey-Bass, 1993). Carnoy incorporates Hirschman's theory of voice in his critique of school choice by emphasizing this activist core of parents. Carnoy argues that "high voice" parents are more likely to opt into choice programs, thereby receiving a better education for their children, though he does not address the potential consequences of this dynamic for control over the public schools. See also Kenneth J. Meier and Kevin B. Smith, *The Case against School Choice: Politics, Markets, and Fools* (Armonk, NY: M.E. Sharpe, 1995).

9. Schneider et al., "Shopping for Schools"; Lawrence F. Feick and Linda L. Price, "The Market Maven: A Diffuser of Marketplace Information," *Journal of Marketing* 51 (1987); Christine H. Roch, "Policy, Networks, and Information: The Role of Opinion Leaders in the Flow of Information about Education" (paper presented at the annual meeting of the American Political Science Association, Washington, DC, August 30–September 2, 2000).

10. Mark Schneider, Paul Teske, Christine Roch, and Melissa Marschall, "Networks to Nowhere: Segregation and Stratification in Networks of Information about Schools," *American Journal of Political Science* 41, no. 4 (1997); Paul E. Teske et al., "Establishing the Micro Foundations of a Macro Theory."

11. Sidney Verba, Kay Lehman Schlozman, and Henry E. Brady, *Voice and Equality.*

12. Terry M. Moe, "Private Vouchers," in Terry M. Moe, ed., *Private Vouchers* (Stanford, CA: Hoover Institution Press, 1995); idem, *Schools, Vouchers, and the American Public* (Washington, DC: Brookings Institution Press, 2001). For a discussion of how problems of stratification may be overcome in public choice programs, see Melissa Marschall, "The Role of Information and Institutional Arrangements in Stemming the Stratifying Effects of School Choice," *Journal of Urban Affairs* 22, no. 3 (2000).

13. Schneider et al., "Networks to Nowhere."

14. Mark Schneider and colleagues (Schneider, Teske, Marschall, Mintrom, and Roch 1997) find significant citizenship benefits to providing choices within a public school system. Though Schneider and colleagues focus on exit within the public sector—which I will do as well in chapter 3 and beyond—the potential social capital–building dynamics are important to voucher programs as well.

15. See James S. Coleman, "Social Capital in the Creation of Human Capital," *American Journal of Sociology* 94 (supplement, 1988).

16. Robert Putnam, *Making Democracy Work: Civic Traditions in Modern Italy* (Princeton: Princeton University Press, 1993); Francis Fukuyama, *Trust: The Social Virtues and the Creation of Prosperity* (New York: Free Press, 1995). Scholars are beginning to examine the effects of school choice on the civic participation and social capital of students. See David E. Campbell, "Making Democratic Education Work," in Peterson and Campbell, eds., *Charters, Vouchers, and Public Education;* Jay P. Greene, "Civic Values in Public and Private Schools," in Paul E. Peterson and Bryan C. Hassel, eds., *Learning from School Choice* (Washington, DC: Brookings Institution Press, 1998). These authors argue that school choice may improve students' civic participation. From the point of view of long-term

development of democratic society, student issues are important; however, from the point of view of effects on how democratic institutions function, parental participation is the appropriate focus.

17. Schneider, Teske, and Marschall, *Choosing Schools.* These authors find evidence that participants in the city's public choice program are more likely to be members of their school's parent-teacher association, participate in school volunteer activities, talk to other parents, and trust their children's teachers than parents of children in assigned public schools. One challenge for Schneider and colleagues is that cross-sectional surveys make it very difficult to establish if participants in the choice programs began with higher levels of participation, if they got that way because they participated in the choice program, or some of both. Though the authors use an instrumental variables technique to control for the possibility of nonrandom assignment, it is difficult to capture what is fundamentally a dynamic process with static data. The larger issue, for the purposes of this chapter, is that the New York City choice program was restricted to choosing between public schools and does not include the private sector. The problem is not whether one would expect similar increases in participation among parents who choose a private option. There is no reason to expect that participation in a choice program that includes private options would not lead to the same kinds of gains for choosers. The issue is which sector, public or private, will benefit from these transformations.

18. To be eligible, families must not have a total household income above 1.75 times the poverty level to participate. The value of the voucher was roughly $3,000 in 1995. As of the 1998–99 school year, religious schools were included in the options, following a change in the legislation.

19. Witte, *The Market Approach to Education.*

20. Data were collected only through the 1994–95 school year and are, unfortunately, no longer being collected (see http://dpls.dacc.wisc.edu/choice/choice_index.html).

21. It is possible, of course, that the different seasons in which the surveys were conducted might affect the results; however, participation questions covered the entire school year, and there is no reason to think a priori that springtime would be correlated with greater school involvement.

22. Witte, *The Market Approach to Education,* 73.

23. Means and standard deviations for all variables included in this chapter are presented in appendix A.

24. Surveys were completed by 1,598 parents in the control group and 252 parents applying for the choice program, of whom 149 were accepted. Of course, some of the parents in the control group also likely applied to the choice program. This possibility, however, means that any differences may actually be stronger than those observed in the analysis. Of the original 1,850 observations 331, or 17 percent, were omitted because of missing values, primarily on the household income variable.

25. Household income is coded on a ten-point scale that is increasing in income. The mean represents an annual income of between $10,000 and $14,999. Parental education is coded on a seven-point scale, increasing in educational attainment. Mother's education is used except where the attainment of fathers is

the only one given. The mean represents a high school graduate. The school contact variable is created by averaging the scores (0–4) on two questions: "How many times during this year did the school contact parent about doing volunteer work and participating in fund-raising?" Each of the two questions was coded 0 for none, 1 for one or two times this year, 2 for three or four times this year, and 3 for five or more times.

26. Verba, Schlozman, and Brady, *Voice and Equality;* Raymond E. Wolfinger and Steven J. Rosenstone, *Who Votes?* (New Haven: Yale University Press, 1980).

27. Gary King, Michael Tomz, and Jason Wittenberg, "Making the Most of Statistical Analysis: Improving Interpretation and Presentation," *American Journal of Political Science* 44, no. 2 (2000).

28. Belonging to the PTA is likely less frequent than participating in its activities as the variable is defined as formal membership, which typically includes paying dues. The membership rates are roughly comparable to national PTA membership rates. See Susan Crawford and Peggy Levitt, "Social Change and Civic Engagement: The Case of the PTA," in Theda Skocpol and Morris P. Fiorina, eds., *Civic Engagement in American Democracy* (Washington, DC: Brookings Institution Press, 1999).

29. This is not to say that PTA membership is always a good thing from the point of view of the schools or that parent-teacher associations always represent the interests of the parent community. The use of PTA instead of a general measure of parental involvement is regrettable in the survey but is useful to indicate differences in participation nonetheless.

30. There are analytical techniques that can be used to attempt to control for attrition bias more systematically; however, these techniques depend on having a vector of personal characteristics to try to impute information about the attrited sample. Unfortunately, the Milwaukee voucher data do not have a sufficient number of these kinds of variables.

31. One might be concerned that the presence of parents of kindergartners in the sample might skew the results, since participation might be expected to be much lower or nonexistent in preschool. However, since acceptance was by lottery, we need not worry about a bias on the key independent variable, since I am concerned about relative differences between the two treatment groups and not on absolute gains. In any case, I repeated the analysis dropping the parents of kindergartners. Substantive conclusions were unchanged.

32. Other coding rules are the same as in table 2.1. Racial and ethnic identification information was not asked in succeeding waves of the survey.

33. Though this analysis focuses only on changes in participation after one year of involvement in the program, I also find some evidence that these gains do hold up over longer periods of time; however, problems of attrition become much more serious the longer one extends the time frame.

34. Because this is a targeted choice program, values of income (and education) for all applicants are substantially lower than the national population's. The lower quartile represents an annual household income of $5,000 or less, the higher quartile $15,000 or greater. All other values set to their means for the purposes of the simulation.

35. The lower quartile of parental education represents less than a high school

diploma, while the higher quartile represents a four-year degree or more. Again, all other values have been set to their means.

36. Verba, Schlozman, and Brady, *Voice and Equality.*

37. John Brehm and Wendy Rahn, "Individual-Level Evidence for the Causes and Consequences of Social Capital," *American Journal of Political Science* 41, no. 3 (1997).

38. Robert Putnam, *Making Democracy Work.*

39. This includes all primary caregivers, including parents, grandparents, and guardians. A total of 9,393 parents participated in this Parent Civic Involvement portion of the survey.

40. For the school participation variable, parents were given one point if they had attended a parent conference at their child's school and one if they had acted as a volunteer at a school event since the beginning of the school year, resulting in a 0 to 2 scale for the school participation variable. For the political participation variable, parents were given one point for having, within the past year, written or telephoned an editor or public official about an issue, attended a public meeting, participated in a community service activity, worked for pay or as a volunteer for a candidate or political party, or participated in a protest or boycott. Household income is divided into 11 income categories, from lowest to highest. Highest degree is coded: 1 = less than high school, 2 = high school or GED, 3 = some college, 4 = college graduate, 5 = graduate school. The means and standard deviations of all variables in this analysis are presented in appendix A.

41. The results of the two regression models are presented in appendix A.

CHAPTER 3

1. Richard F. Fenno Jr., *Watching Politicians: Essays on Participant Observation* (Berkeley, CA: IGS Press, 1990), 2.

2. It should be noted that the principal was not yet facing and not expecting a charter school at the high school level, possibly increasing his confidence. Given my small number of observational subjects, the comparative question is left unexplored.

3. James S. Coleman et al., *Equality of Educational Opportunity* (Washington, DC: U.S. GPO, 1966).

4. Fenno, *Watching Politicians,* 114. Italics are Fenno's.

5. Fenno, *Watching Politicians,* vii.

6. I did not use a tape recorder but made notes during the meetings, briefings, and debriefings and reviewed and supplemented these notes immediately following each encounter.

7. Richard F. Fenno Jr., *Home Style: House Members in Their Districts* (HarperCollins Publishers, 1978), 254.

8. Jane Hannaway, *Managers Managing: The Workings of an Administrative System* (New York: Oxford University Press, 1989).

9. Frederick M. Hess, "Hints of the Pick-Axe"; idem, *Revolution at the Margins* (Washington, DC: Brookings Institution Press, 2002); Frederick M. Hess,

Robert Maranto, and Scott Milliman, "Responding to Competition: School Leaders and School Culture," in Peterson and Campbell, eds., *Charters, Vouchers, and Public Education;* Michael Mintrom and David N. Plank, "School Choice in Michigan," in Peterson and Campbell, eds., *Charters, Vouchers, and Public Education;* Thomas T. Holyoke and Jeffrey R. Henig, "All for One or Each for Its Own?"

10. Jean Rimbach, "Funding Lacks for First Charter Schools, Survey Finds," *(Bergen) Record,* June 10, 1998.

11. Kathleen Cannon, "Whitman Defends Charter School Record while Critics Call for More Oversight," *Associated Press State and Local Wire,* September 9, 2000.

12. Of course, teachers, as union members, can advocate, negotiate, and mobilize for new contracts.

13. I am currently undertaking a research project on the effects of the simultaneous implementation of centralization and decentralization reforms on the public schools. These effects, however, are beyond the scope of this study.

14. Hirschman, *Exit, Voice, and Loyalty,* 31. See also John R. Hibbing and Elizabeth Theiss-Morse, "The Perils of Voice: Political Involvement's Potential to Delegitimate" (paper presented at the annual meeting of the American Political Science Association, Boston, August 29–September 1, 2002).

15. New Jersey School Boards Association, press release, Trenton, April 19.

16. Ibid.

17. Mancur Olson, *The Logic of Collective Action.*

CHAPTER 4

1. F. Howard Nelson, Bella Rosenberg, and Nancy Van Meter, "Charter School Achievement on the 2003 National Assessment of Educational Progress" (American Federation of Teachers, AFL-CIO, 2004).

2. Gary Miron and Christopher Nelson, "Student Academic Achievement in Charter Schools: What We Know and Why We Know So Little," National Center for the Study of Privatization in Education, Teachers College, Columbia University, Occasional Paper Number 41 (2001).

3. Chester E. Finn, Bruno V. Manno, and Greg Vanourek, *Charter Schools in Action: Renewing Public Education* (Princeton: Princeton University Press, 2000); Stella Cheung, Mary Ellen Murphy, and Joe Nathan, "Making a Difference? Charter Schools, Evaluation, and Student Performance," Center for School Change, University of Minnesota (1998).

4. Many Minnesota public school students have the opportunity to choose schools in adjacent districts. While these programs also provide competitive pressures on the public schools, the focus for this project is on the effects of the statewide charter school legislation.

5. Frederick M. Hess, *Revolution at the Margins;* Eric Rofes, *How Are School Districts Responding to Charter Laws and Charter Schools? A Study of Eight States and the District of Columbia* (Berkeley: University of California at Berkeley Policy Analysis for California Education, 1998).

6. Frederick M. Hess, "Hints of the Pick-Axe."

7. Frederick M. Hess, Robert Maranto, and Scott Milliman, "Responding to Competition."

8. Paul E. Teske et al., "Can Charter Schools Change Traditional Public Schools?" in Peterson and Campbell, eds., *Charters, Vouchers, and Public Education,* 200; Paul E. Teske and Mark Schneider, *The Importance of Leadership: The Role of School Principals* (Arlington, VA: PricewaterhouseCoopers Endowment for the Business of Government, 1999). For a contrary perspective on these footsteps, see Lorna Jimmerson, "Hidden Consequences of School Choice: Impact on Programs, Finances, and Accountability" (paper presented at the annual meeting of the American Educational Research Association, San Diego, April 13–17, 1998).

9. Paul T. Hill and Robin J. Lake, *Charter Schools and Accountability in Public Education* (Washington, DC: Brookings Institution Press, 2002), 36.

10. Jack Buckley, Simona Kúcsová, and Mark Schneider, "Building Social Capital in the Nation's Capital: Can Charter Schools Build a Foundation for Cooperative Behavior?" (paper presented at the annual meeting of the American Political Science Association, Philadelphia, August 28–31, 2003).

11. Ibid. Their approach takes seriously the policy feedback literature discussed in chapter 1, by considering the dynamic of charter school reforms and "citizen attitudes toward government and their willingness to participate in politics and the policy process" (2). Still, as theirs is an ongoing panel study in its early stages, these patterns may change in the future.

12. This research was made possible through a Faculty Interactive Research Program grant from the Center for Urban and Regional Affairs at the University of Minnesota and in association with the university's Minnesota Center for Survey Research. Portions of this chapter were previously published as Scott F. Abernathy, "Charter Schools, Parents, and Public Schools in Minnesota," *CURA Reporter* 34 (winter 2004): 1–7 (available from the University of Minnesota's Center for Urban and Regional Affairs, www.cura.umn.edu).

13. This is not as precise a measure of competition as I would like. However, measuring competition by the presence of a charter school in the district with students at the same grade level as the equivalent noncharter school raises its own problems. It would disallow ungraded charter schools or those with grade levels that do not coincide with traditional schools' and would not allow for expected future expansion of charter schools, which is part of the plan in most cases. I caution my readers nonetheless.

14. Randall W. Eberts and Joe A. Stone, "Student Achievement in Public Schools: Do Principals Make a Difference?" *Economics of Education Review* 7, no. 3 (1988).

15. Jane Hannaway, "The Organization and Management of Public and Catholic Schools: Looking inside the 'Black Box,'" *International Journal of Educational Research* 15 (1991); idem, "Political Pressure and Decentralization: The Case of School Districts," *Sociology of Education* 66, no. 3 (1993).

16. Chubb and Moe, *Politics, Markets, and America's Schools.*

17. The models include a variable indicating if the principal has at least ten years of experience, another indicating that the principal has taught for at least ten

years, and another indicating if the principal has earned a Ph.D. or equivalent degree. Measures of the principal's race, ethnicity, or gender are not included in these models because I have no theoretical reason to include them (unlike with community demographic characteristics) and because in none of the analyses of this chapter do individual identity variables affect the substantive conclusions when one cannot reject the null that the identity variables add no explanatory power to the models.

18. The number of students, the highest grade offered in the school (or whether it is an ungraded school), and the percentage of students in the school who are Hispanic, African American, eligible for free lunch programs, or classified as limited English proficient. School-level demographic data come from the Minnesota Department of Education's Fall Populations by School 2002–2003 and Gender by Ethnicity by School 2002–2003.

19. I repeated each analysis after deleting Minneapolis and St. Paul schools from the sample to verify that characteristics unique to the Twin Cities were not driving the results (since every public school principal in the Twin Cities is, at least theoretically, faced with a charter school). In all cases, the substantive conclusions were unchanged, and, in fact, many standard error estimates were reduced.

20. The coefficient estimates on the effects of parents on principals' influence in establishing curriculum and setting discipline policy, though showing similar patterns, are not presented as one cannot reject the null hypothesis of poor goodness of fit.

21. All variables that are not dichotomous are set at their mean values. Each dichotomous variable are set at the value that corresponds to the majority of respondents, which is associated with principals that have less than ten years' experience as a principal and no Ph.D. or equivalent, but ten or more years' experience as a teacher.

22. The regression results are presented in appendix B.

23. Though principals in charter school districts report spending less time on facilities and principals in charter school districts report spending more time on administrative tasks (both of which are significant at the 0.10 level, two-tailed), these results are not included due to the same concerns about goodness of fit as before.

24. Readers should note that most principals reported offering these options to parents. Of interest, however, is not the level of participation principals reported offering to parents, but rather if there are meaningful differences among the three types of schools in the opportunities available for parents to participate.

25. In their study of public school choice, Mark Schneider, Paul Teske, and Melissa Marschall note that though "choice is capable of unleashing forces that can have positive effects on parents, schools, and communities . . . choice is not operating in a vacuum." Schneider, Teske, and Marschall, *Choosing Schools,* 4.

26. Full results are presented in appendix B.

27. Hirschman, *Exit, Voice, and Loyalty,* 45.

28. I do not have survey evidence from Minnesota school parents to confirm the changes in attitudes and trust associated with social capital–building processes. However, there is no reason to think that making choices in private education is significantly different from making choices in public education.

29. My thanks to an anonymous reviewer for clarification of this point.

30. Schneider, Teske, and Marschall conclude the same thing about public school choice. Schneider, Teske, and Marschall, *Choosing Schools,* 261.

CHAPTER 5

1. V. O. Key Jr., *Public Opinion and American Democracy* (New York: Alfred A. Knopf, 1961), 229.

2. New Jersey has two types of governance structures for school districts, based on how school board members are chosen. In Type I districts, the mayor appoints the board members, and the district residents do not get to vote on the base budgets. In Type II districts, board members are elected, and residents are allowed to vote on school budgets. Any district can change its status by putting the question on a municipal ballot. As of 2002, seventeen of New Jersey's school boards are appointed. The remainder of the 10 percent of nonvoting districts consists of special vocational districts, special services districts, educational service commissions, and nonoperating districts that send their students to schools in other districts. Cindy Tietjen, "Small Number of State's School Districts Have Appointed Boards," *Tri-Town News,* September 17, 2002.

3. New Jersey School Boards Association, press release (Trenton, April 11, 2001).

4. New Jersey School Boards Association, press release (Trenton, April 21, 1999).

5. Ibid.

6. Thomas Romer and Howard Rosenthal, "Bureaucrats versus Voters: On the Political Economy of Resource Action by Direct Democracy," *Quarterly Journal of Economics* 93, no. 4 (1979).

7. Sidney Verba, Kay Lehman Schlozman, and Henry E. Brady, *Voice and Equality.*

8. Though there have been calls to move the budget elections to the fall to improve turnout, the fact that elections are held by themselves in the spring is empirically useful here, as one does not need to worry about the effects of other elections on the results.

9. In 2002, only 15,605 out of New Jersey's 1.3 million students were attending charter schools (New Jersey Department of Education, Vital Statistics).

10. My thanks to an anonymous reviewer for clarification of this point. See. J. Eric Oliver, *Democracy in Suburbia* (Princeton: Princeton University Press, 2001), which finds that economic segregation reduces citizen involvement with government.

CHAPTER 6

1. John Dewey, *Democracy and Education* (New York: Free Press, 1916), 248.

2. Alexis de Tocqueville, *Democracy in America,* translated by Gerald E. Bevan (1835; repr. Penguin Books, 2003), 592.

3. See Brehm and Rahn, "Individual-Level Evidence for the Causes and Consequences of Social Capital"; Clarence N. Stone et al., *Building Civic Capacity*. Stone and colleagues assert that the loss of activist parental voices to the suburbs need not "create a destiny of failure" (73) but requires a conscious effort to revitalize democratic participation in these drained communities. See also Clarence N. Stone, "Introduction: Urban Education in a Political Context," and "Civic Capacity and Urban School Reform," in Clarence N. Stone, ed., *Changing Urban Education* (Lawrence: University Press of Kansas, 1998).

4. I encourage future researchers to conduct systematic studies of the potentially beneficial effects of competition from private schools on the customer awareness, outreach, and programmatic responses in the public schools in cities (and states) with voucher programs in operation.

5. I am grateful to an anonymous reviewer for clarification of this point.

6. Jennifer L. Hochschild and Michael N. Danielson, "Can We Desegregate Public Schools and Subsidized Housing? Lessons from the Sorry History of Yonkers, New York," in Clarence N. Stone, ed., *Changing Urban Education* (Lawrence: University Press of Kansas, 1998). Hochschild and Danielson argue that the hope for an apolitical education is an obstacle to real reform.

7. Eric A. Hanushek, "Measuring Investment in Education," *Journal of Economic Perspectives* 10, no. 4 (1996).

8. Clarence Stone and his colleagues acknowledge this point: "Fiscal capacity is a necessary but insufficient condition for educational reform." *Building Civic Capacity,* 69.

9. Stone et al., *Building Civic Capacity.*

10. Campbell does not fully explore this, as this is not her primary concern.

11. Mobilizing middle-class and poor parents together could be a major first step in closing the participation gap between the young and the old that Campbell observes.

12. Charles E. Lindblom, *Politics and Markets* (New York: Basic Books, 1977), 358.

13. I am grateful to an anonymous reviewer for clarification of this point.

14. This section draws heavily on the ideas of Charles Lindblom, Robert Dahl, and Jennifer Hochschild, though none of these scholars had the same concerns with issues of liberty and equality in policy design and implementation that I explore here. For a nice discussion of liberty and equality in public and private educational systems, see Witte, *The Market Approach to Education,* 13.

15. Alexis de Tocqueville (1835) noted that liberty and equality were bound together, though he also noted the virtues of channeling the pursuit of individual liberty through the democratic process.

16. See, for example, William F. Russell, "So Conceived and So Dedicated," *Annals of the American Academy of Political and Social Science* 180 (1935). In the current debate, John Witte explores this tension in detail in *The Market Approach to Education.*

17. These charges are sometimes laid against public schools, which do not display equal educational outcomes but restrict choice at the same time. See Witte, *The Market Approach to Education,* 18.

18. Alexis de Tocqueville (1835) noted that equality and liberty, properly pur-

sued, are mutually self-reinforcing. See Kathryn A. McDermott, *Controlling for Public Education: Localism versus Equity* (Lawrence: University Press of Kansas, 1999). McDermott reaches a similar conclusion about the need to centralize resource allocation and decentralize governance, in this case, as a response to the failings of local control to preserve equality and mitigate segregation.

19. Chubb and Moe, *Politics, Markets, and America's Schools*, 215–26; Jeffrey Henig, *Rethinking School Choice*, 86–90.

20. Perhaps the reason for the dearth of attention was that the plan was extraordinarily ambitious. The authors noted this themselves. Chubb and Moe, *Politics, Markets, and America's Schools*, 226.

21. Religious schools would be free to become public schools in their plan. I am wary of this, largely because of the prospect of creeping government regulation of religion.

22. There is much in my plan that sounds suspiciously European. True. The lack of comparisons with European educational systems is, I believe, one of the main weaknesses of this book; however, there is only so much that I can do. I encourage other scholars to draw these comparisons, and I note that—in all the hand-wringing about the decline of American education—European countries are the ones that tend to do well on these international comparisons.

23. Chubb and Moe do not go into much detail on how transportation issues would be resolved. Nor do I. It is clear, however, that the challenges to many rural students could be significant.

24. Stone et al., *Building Civic Capacity*, 57.

25. Actually, the program would be implemented by state governments, given the lack of a federal constitutional promise of education. But fiscal statism sounds kind of misleading.

References

Bendor, Jonathan, and Terry M. Moe. 1985. "An Adaptive Model of Bureaucratic Politics." *American Political Science Review* 79 (3): 755–74.

Bernheim, B. Douglas, and Michael D. Whinston. 1986. "Common Agency." *Econometrica* 54 (4): 923–42.

Brady, Henry E., Sidney Verba, and Kay Lehman Schlozman. 1995. "Beyond SES: A Resource Model of Political Participation." *American Political Science Review* 89 (2): 271–94.

Brehm, John, and Wendy Rahn. 1997. "Individual-Level Evidence for the Causes and Consequences of Social Capital." *American Journal of Political Science* 41 (3): 999–1023.

Buckley, Jack, Simona Kúcsová, and Mark Schneider. 2003. "Building Social Capital in the Nation's Capital: Can Charter Schools Build a Foundation for Cooperative Behavior?" Paper presented at the annual meeting of the American Political Science Association, Philadelphia, August 28–31.

Campbell, Andrea Louise. 2002. "Self-Interest, Social Security, and the Distinctive Participation Patterns of Seniors." *American Political Science Review* 96 (3): 565–74.

———. 2003. *How Policies Make Citizens.* Princeton: Princeton University Press.

Campbell, David E. 2001. "Making Democratic Education Work." In *Charters, Vouchers, and Public Education,* edited by Paul E. Peterson and David E. Campbell. Washington, DC: Brookings Institution Press.

Cannon, Kathleen. 2000. "Whitman Defends Charter School Record While Critics Call for More Oversight." *Associated Press State & Local Wire,* September 9.

Carnoy, Martin. 1993. "School Improvement: Is Privatization the Answer?" In *Decentralization and School Improvement,* edited by Jane Hannaway and Martin Carnoy. San Francisco: Jossey-Bass.

Chesler, Mark A., Bunyant I. Bryant, and James E. Crowfoot. 1981. *Making Desegregation Work: A Professional's Guide to Effecting Change.* Beverly Hills, CA: Sage Publications.

Cheung, Stella, Mary Ellen Murphy, and Joe Nathan. 1998. "Making a Difference? Charter Schools, Evaluation, and Student Performance." Center for School Change, University of Minnesota.

Chubb, John E., and Terry M. Moe. 1990. *Politics, Markets, and America's Schools.* Washington, DC: Brookings Institution Press.

Coleman, James S. 1988. "Social Capital in the Creation of Human Capital."
    American Journal of Sociology 94 (Supplement): S95–120.
Coleman, James S., E. Q. Campbell, C. J. Hobson, J. McPortland, A. M. Mood,
    F. D. Weinfeld, and R. L. York. 1966. *Equality of Educational Opportunity.*
    Washington, DC: U.S. GPO.
Coleman, James S., Thomas Hoffer, and Sally Kilgore. 1982. *High School Achieve-*
    ment. New York: Basic Books.
Crawford, Susan, and Peggy Levitt. 1999. "Social Change and Civic Engagement:
    The Case of the PTA." In *Civic Engagement in American Democracy,* edited by
    Theda Skocpol and Morris P. Fiorina. Washington, DC: Brookings Institution
    Press.
Dahl, Robert A. 1985. *A Preface to Economic Democracy.* Berkeley: University of
    California Press.
Dewey, John. 1916. *Democracy and Education.* New York: Free Press.
Dixit, Avinash. 1997. "Power of Incentives in Private versus Public Organiza-
    tions." *American Economic Review* 87 (2): 378–82.
Dixit, Avinash, Gene M. Grossman, and Elhanan Helpman. 1997. "Common
    Agency and Coordination: General Theory and Application to Government
    Policy Making." *Journal of Political Economy* 105 (4): 752–69.
Eberts, Randall W., and Joe A. Stone. 1988. "Student Achievement in Public
    Schools: Do Principals Make a Difference?" *Economics of Education Review* 7
    (3): 291–99.
Feick, Lawrence F., and Linda L. Price. 1987. "The Market Maven: A Diffuser of
    Marketplace Information." *Journal of Marketing* 51:83–97.
Fenno, Richard F., Jr. 1978. *Home Style: House Members in Their Districts.*
    Boston: Little, Brown.
———. 1990. *Watching Politicians: Essays on Participant Observation.* Berkeley,
    CA: IGS Press.
Finn, Chester E., Bruno V. Manno, and Greg Vanourek. 2000. *Charter Schools in*
    Action: Renewing Public Education. Princeton: Princeton University Press.
Friedman, Milton. 1955. "The Role of Government in Education." In *Economics*
    and the Public Interest, edited by Robert A. Solo. New Brunswick, NJ: Rutgers
    University Press.
Fukuyama, Francis. 1995. *Trust: The Social Virtues and the Creation of Prosperity.*
    New York: Free Press.
Garner, William T., and Jane Hannaway. 1982. "Private Schools: The Client Con-
    nection." In *Family Choice in Schooling,* edited by Michael E. Manley-Casimir.
    Lexington, MA: Lexington Books.
Gaventa, John. 1980. *Power and Powerlessness: Quiescence and Rebellion in an*
    Appalachian Valley. Urbana: University of Illinois Press.
Godwin, R. Kenneth, and Frank R. Kemerer. 2002. *School Choice Tradeoffs: Lib-*
    erty, Equity, and Diversity. Austin: University of Texas Press.
Greene, Jay P. 1998. "Civic Values in Public and Private Schools." In *Learning*
    from School Choice, edited by Paul E. Peterson and Bryan C. Hassel. Washing-
    ton, DC: Brookings Institution Press.
Hacker, Jacob, Suzanne Mettler, Dianne Pinderhughes, and Theda Skocpol. 2004.

"Inequality and Public Policy." Task Force Report on Inequality and American Democracy. American Political Science Association.

Hannaway, Jane. 1989. *Managers Managing: The Workings of an Administrative System*. New York: Oxford University Press.

———. 1991. "The Organization and Management of Public and Catholic Schools: Looking inside the 'Black Box.'" *International Journal of Educational Research* 15:463–81.

———. 1993. "Political Pressure and Decentralization: The Case of School Districts." *Sociology of Education* 66 (3): 147–63.

Hanushek, Eric A. 1996. "Measuring Investment in Education." *Journal of Economic Perspectives* 10 (4): 9–30.

Henig, Jeffrey. 1994. *Rethinking School Choice: Limits of the Market Metaphor*. Princeton: Princeton University Press.

Hess, Frederick M. 2001. "Hints of the Pick-Axe: Competition and Public Schooling in Milwaukee." In *Charters, Vouchers, and Public Education*, edited by Paul E. Peterson and David E. Campbell. Washington, DC: Brookings Institution Press.

———. 2002. *Revolution at the Margins*. Washington, DC: Brookings Institution Press.

Hess, Frederick, Robert Maranto, and Scott Milliman. 2001. "Responding to Competition: School Leaders and School Culture." In *Charters, Vouchers, and Public Education*, edited by Paul E. Peterson and David E. Campbell. Washington, DC: Brookings Institution Press.

Hibbing, John R., and Elizabeth Theiss-Morse. 2002. "The Perils of Voice: Political Involvement's Potential to Delegitimate." Paper presented at the annual meeting of the American Political Science Association, Boston, August 29–September 1.

Hill, Paul T., and Robin J. Lake. 2002. *Charter Schools and Accountability in Public Education*. Washington, DC: Brookings Institution Press.

Hirschman, Albert O. 1970. *Exit, Voice, and Loyalty: Responses to Decline in Firms, Organizations, and States*. Cambridge, MA: Harvard University Press.

Hochschild, Jennifer L. 1984. *The New American Dilemma: Liberal Democracy and School Desegregation*. New Haven: Yale University Press.

Hochschild, Jennifer L., and Michael N. Danielson. 1998. "Can We Desegregate Public Schools and Subsidized Housing? Lessons from the Sorry History of Yonkers, New York." In *Changing Urban Education*, edited by Clarence N. Stone. Lawrence: University Press of Kansas.

Hochschild, Jennifer L., and Nathan Scovronick. 2003. *The American Dream and the Public Schools*. New York: Oxford University Press.

Holyoke, Thomas T., and Jeffrey R. Henig. 2001. "All for One or Each for Its Own? Charter Schools and Collective Action in the District of Columbia." Paper presented at the annual meeting of the Midwest Political Science Association, Chicago, April 19–22.

Howell, William G., and Paul E. Peterson (with Patrick J. Wolf, and David E. Campbell). 2002. *The Educational Gap: Vouchers and Urban Schools*. Washington, DC: Brookings Institution Press.

Howell, William G., Patrick J. Wolf, Paul E. Peterson, and David E. Campbell. 2001. "Effects of School Choice on Test Scores." In *Charters, Vouchers, and Public Education,* edited by Paul E. Peterson and David E. Campbell. Washington, DC: Brookings Institution Press.

Jimerson, Lorna. 1998. "Hidden Consequences of School Choice: Impact on Programs, Finances, and Accountability." Presented at the annual meeting of the American Educational Research Association, San Diego, April 13–17.

Key, V. O., Jr. 1961. *Public Opinion and American Democracy.* New York: Alfred A. Knopf.

King, Gary, Michael Tomz, and Jason Wittenberg. 2000. "Making the Most of Statistical Analysis: Improving Interpretation and Presentation." *American Journal of Political Science* 44 (2): 341–55.

Krueger, Alan B., and Pei Zhu. 2004a. "Another Look at the New York City School Voucher Experiment." *American Behavioral Scientist* 47 (5): 658–98.

———. 2004b. "Inefficiency, Subsample Selection Bias, and Nonrobustness: A Response to Paul E. Peterson and William G. Howell." *American Behavioral Scientist* 47 (5): 718—28.

Levin, Henry M. 1998. "Educational Vouchers: Effectiveness, Choice, and Costs." *Journal of Policy Analysis and Management* 17 (3): 373–92.

Lindblom, Charles E. 1977. *Politics and Markets: The World's Political Economic Systems.* New York: Basic Books.

Mansbridge, Jane J. 1990. "The Rise and Fall of Self-Interest in the Explanation of Political Life." In *Beyond Self-Interest,* edited by Jane J. Mansbridge. Chicago: University of Chicago Press.

Marschall, Melissa. 2000. "The Role of Information and Institutional Arrangements in Stemming the Stratifying Effects of School Choice." *Journal of Urban Affairs* 22 (3): 333–50.

McDermott, Kathryn A. 1999. *Controlling Public Education: Localism versus Equity.* Lawrence: University Press of Kansas.

McGrath, Mary. 1994. "Coalition Backs School Voucher Proposal." *(Bergen) Record,* October 12.

Meier, Kenneth J., and Kevin B. Smith. 1995. *The Case against School Choice: Politics, Markets, and Fools.* Armonk, NY: M. E. Sharpe.

Mettler, Suzanne. 2002. "Bringing the State Back In to Civic Engagement: Policy Feedback Effects of the G.I. Bill for World War II Veterans." *American Political Science Review* 96 (2): 351–65.

———. Forthcoming. *Civic Generation: The G.I. Bill in Veterans' Lives.* Oxford University Press.

Mettler, Suzanne, and Joe Soss. 2004. "The Consequences of Public Policy for Democratic Citizenship: Bridging Policy Studies and Mass Politics." *Perspectives on Politics* 2 (1): 55–73.

Minnesota Department of Education. 2003a. "Fall Populations by School: 2002–03." (http://cfl.state.mn.us/datactr/fallpops/index.htm).

———. 2003b. "Gender by Ethnicity by School: 2002–03." (http://cfl.state.mn.us/datactr/enroll/index.htm).

Mintrom, Michael, and David N. Plank. 2001. "School Choice in Michigan." In

Charters, Vouchers, and Public Education, edited by Paul E. Peterson and David E. Campbell. Washington, DC: Brookings Institution Press.

Miron, Gary, and Christopher Nelson. 2001. "Student Academic Achievement in Charter Schools: What We Know and Why We Know So Little." National Center for the Study of Privatization in Education, Teachers College, Columbia University, Occasional Paper Number 41.

Moe, Terry M. 1984. "The New Economics of Organization." *American Journal of Political Science* 28 (4): 739–77.

———. 1995. "Private Vouchers." In *Private Vouchers,* edited by Terry M. Moe. Stanford, CA: Hoover Institution Press.

———. 2001. *Schools, Vouchers, and the American Public.* Washington, DC: Brookings Institution Press.

Moynihan, Daniel P. 1969. *Maximum Feasible Misunderstanding: Community Action in the War on Poverty.* New York: Free Press.

Nelson, F. Howard, Bella Rosenberg, and Nancy Van Meter. 2004. "Charter School Achievement on the 2003 National Assessment of Educational Progress." American Federation of Teachers, AFL-CIO.

New Jersey Legislative District Data Book. 1996–2003. New Brunswick, NJ: Edward J. Bloustein School of Planning and Policy, Center for Government Services.

New Jersey School Boards Association. 1999. Press release, Trenton. April 21.

———. 2000. Press release, Trenton. April 19.

———. 2001. Press release, Trenton. April 11.

New York Times. 1994. "New Jersey's New Governor: Excerpts from Whitman's Address on Leadership, Taxes, and Schools." January 19, B4.

Oliver, J. Eric. 2001. *Democracy in Suburbia.* Princeton: Princeton University Press.

Olson, Mancur. 1971. *The Logic of Collective Action: Public Goods and the Theory of Groups.* Cambridge, MA: Harvard University Press.

Peterson, Paul E., and William G. Howell. 2004. "Efficiency, Bias, and Classification Schemes: A Response to Alan B. Krueger and Pei Zhu." *American Behavioral Scientist* 47 (5): 699–717.

Pierson, Paul. 1993. "When Effect Becomes Cause: Policy Feedback and Political Change." *World Politics* 45:595–628.

Pressman, Jeffrey L., and Aaron Wildavsky. 1984. *Implementation: How Great Expectations in Washington Are Dashed in Oakland.* Berkeley: University of California Press.

Putnam, Robert. 1993. *Making Democracy Work: Civic Traditions in Modern Italy.* Princeton: Princeton University Press.

Rein, Martin. 1989. "The Social Structure of Institutions: Neither Public nor Private." In *Privatization and the Welfare State,* edited by Sheila B. Kamerman and Alfred J. Kahn. Princeton: Princeton University Press.

Rimbach, Jean. 1998. "Funding Lacks for First Charter Schools, Survey Finds." *(Bergen) Record,* June 10, A04.

Roch, Christine H. 2000. "Policy, Networks, and Information: The Role of Opinion Leaders in the Flow of Information about Education." Paper presented at the annual meeting of the American Political Science Association, Washington, DC, August 30–September 2.

Rofes, Eric. 1998. *How Are School Districts Responding to Charter Laws and Charter Schools? A Study of Eight States and the District of Columbia.* Berkeley: University of California at Berkeley Policy Analysis for California Education.

Romer, Thomas, and Howard Rosenthal. 1979. "Bureaucrats versus Voters: On the Political Economy of Resource Action by Direct Democracy." *Quarterly Journal of Economics* 93 (4): 563–67.

Ross, Stephen A. 1973. "The Economic Theory of Agency: The Principal's Problem." *American Economic Review* 63 (2): 134–39.

Rouse, Cecilia Elena. 1998. "Schools and Student Achievement: More Evidence from the Milwaukee Parental Choice Program." *Federal Reserve Bank of New York Economic Policy Review* 61–76.

Russell, William F. 1935. "So Conceived and So Dedicated." *Annals of the American Academy of Political and Social Science* 180:168–75.

Schattschneider, E. E. 1935. *Politics, Pressures, and the Tariff.* New York: Prentice-Hall.

Schneider, Anne, and Helen Ingram. 1993. "Social Construction of Target Populations: Implications for Politics and Policy." *American Political Science Review* 87 (2): 334–47.

Schneider, Mark, Paul Teske, and Melissa Marschall. 2000. *Choosing Schools: Consumer Choice and the Quality of American Education.* Princeton: Princeton University Press.

Schneider, Mark, Paul Teske, Melissa Marschall, Michael Mintrom, and Christine Roch. 1997. "Institutional Arrangements and the Creation of Social Capital: The Effects of Public School Choice." *American Political Science Review* 91 (1): 82–93.

Schneider, Mark, Paul Teske, Melissa Marschall, and Christine Roch. 1998. "Shopping for Schools: In the Land of the Blind, the One-Eyed Parent May Be Enough." *American Journal of Political Science* 42 (3): 769–93.

Schneider, Mark, Paul Teske, Christine Roch, and Melissa Marschall. 1997. "Networks to Nowhere: Segregation and Stratification in Networks of Information about Schools." *American Journal of Political Science* 41 (4): 1201–23.

Skocpol, Theda. 1992. *Protecting Soldiers and Mothers: The Political Origins of Social Policy in the United States.* Cambridge, MA: Harvard University Press.

———. 2003. *Diminished Democracy: From Membership to Management in American Civic Life.* Norman: University of Oklahoma Press.

Skowronek, Stephen. 1982. *Building a New American State: The Expansion of National Administrative Capacities, 1877–1920.* New York: Cambridge University Press.

Soss, Joe. 1999. "Lessons of Welfare: Policy Design, Political Learning, and Political Action." *American Political Science Review* 93 (2): 363–80.

Stone, Clarence N. 1998a. "Introduction: Urban Education in a Political Context." In *Changing Urban Education,* edited by Clarence N. Stone. Lawrence: University Press of Kansas.

———. 1998b. "Civic Capacity and Urban School Reform." In *Changing Urban Education,* edited by Clarence N. Stone. Lawrence: University Press of Kansas.

Stone, Clarence N., Jeffrey R. Henig, Bryan D. Jones, and Carol Peirannunzi. 2001. *Building Civic Capacity: The Politics of Reforming Urban Schools.* Lawrence: University Press of Kansas.

Teske, Paul E., and Mark Schneider. 1999. *The Importance of Leadership: The Role of School Principals.* Arlington, VA: PricewaterhouseCoopers Endowment for the Business of Government.

Teske, Paul E., Mark Schneider, Sara Clark, and Jack Buckley. 2001. "Can Charter Schools Change Traditional Public Schools?" In *Charters, Vouchers, and Public Education,* edited by Paul E. Peterson and David E. Campbell. Washington, DC: Brookings Institution Press.

Teske, Paul E., Mark Schneider, Michael Mintrom, and Samuel Best. 1993. "Establishing the Micro Foundations of a Macro Theory: Information Movers and the Competitive Local Market for Public Goods." *American Political Science Review* 87 (3): 702–13.

Tietjen, Cindy. 2002. "Small Number of State's School Districts Have Appointed Boards." *Tri-Town News,* September 17.

Tocqueville, Alexis de. [1835] 2003. *Democracy in America.* Translated by Gerald E. Bevan. Penguin Books.

United States Department of Education. National Center for Education Statistics. 1995. *1993–94 Schools and Staffing Survey: Data File User's Manual.* Washington, DC.

———. 1997. *National Household Education Survey of 1996: Data File User's Manual,* volumes 1–6, NCES 97–425. Washington, DC.

United States General Accounting Office. 2001. "School Vouchers: Publicly Funded Programs in Cleveland and Milwaukee." *Report to the Honorable Judd Gregg, U.S. Senate.* Washington, DC.

———. 2002. "Insufficient Research to Determine Effectiveness of Selected Private Education Companies." *Report to the Ranking Minority Member, Subcommittee on the District of Columbia, Committee on Appropriations, House of Representatives.* Washington, DC.

Verba, Sidney, Kay Lehman Schlozman, and Henry E. Brady. 1995. *Voice and Equality: Civic Volunteerism in American Politics.* Cambridge, MA: Harvard University Press.

Witte, John F. 1998. "The Milwaukee Voucher Experiment." *Educational Evaluation and Policy Analysis* 20:229–52.

———. 2000. *The Market Approach to Education: An Analysis of America's First Voucher Program.* Princeton: Princeton University Press.

Witte, John F., and Christopher A. Thorn. 1995. *The Milwaukee Parental Choice Program 1990/1991–1994/1995* (computer file). Madison, WI: John F. Witte and Christopher A. Thorn (producers), 1995, Madison, WI: Data and Program Library Service (distributor), 1995; http://dpls.dacc.wisc.edu/choice/choice_index.html (accessed June 14, 1999).

Wolfinger, Raymond E., and Steven J. Rosenstone. 1980. *Who Votes?* New Haven: Yale University Press.

Index

academic achievement and: charter schools, 73–74; school choice, 8; voucher programs, 22–23

Advanced Placement, 64–65

agency, common, 11, 60, 71

Building Civic Capacity (Stone et al.), 6–7

bureaucratic responsiveness: charter schools and, 2, 74–76, 80–85; common agency and, 11, 60–63; market forces and, 2–4; school choice and, 2, 3–4, 10, 15, 74–75, 102, 116

Campbell, Andrea Louise, 14, 109

Carnoy, Martin, 136–37n8

charter schools: compared to voucher programs, 18, 86–87, 105–6; defined, 1–2, 16–17, 73; funding of, 2, 67; in Minnesota, 76; in New Jersey, 1–2, 55–57; observational studies of principals in, 52–54; parental satisfaction with, 73–74; social capital formation and, 75; statistical analyses of, in Minnesota, 121–27; unfair competition and, 2, 67–68

charter schools, effects on: academic achievement, 73–74; bureaucratic responsiveness, 2, 74–76, 80–85; parental participation, 84–85; principals' views of parents, 76–80; school budget approval, 97–100; skimming of active parents and, 66–67; voter turnout, 94–97

Chubb, John E.: advocacy of parental choice, 3–4; Chubb and Moe scholarship plan, 112; on failures of public education, 7, 9; findings of, critiqued, 4, 18–19, 112; findings of, supported, 80, 86, 102, 107–8

civic capacity, 6–7, 109

civic mobilization, 6–7

Cleveland, OH, 8, 21–22

client connection, 9–10

Columbia University Teachers College, 57

cross-class coalitions: in education, 109, 116; fully funded choice and, 114, 115; parent-teacher organizations and, 13–14; social security and, 13–14, 109

customers: active subset of, 5, 23–24; exit of, 5–6

Dahl, Robert, 4–5, 18, 145n14

Danielson, Michael N., 145n6

democracy: bureaucratic consequences of, 3, 110–11; effects of markets on, 4–5, 18–19, 111

Democracy and Education (Dewey), 101

Democracy in America (Tocqueville), 101

Dewey, John, 101

Diminished Democracy (Skocpol), 13–14

educational choice. See school choice

155